CIVIL LIBERTIES IN ENGLAND AND WALES

CIVIL LIBERTIES IN ENGLAND AND WALES

Essays

S.R.DABYDEEN

iUniverse, Inc.
New York Lincoln Shanghai

CIVIL LIBERTIES IN ENGLAND AND WALES
Essays

iUniverse, Inc.

For information address:
iUniverse, Inc.
2021 Pine Lake Road, Suite 100
Lincoln, NE 68512
www.iuniverse.com

This book is not intended as a source of advice to any person. The author does not accept any responsibility for anything that any person does or does not do as a result of reading this book. The law in this book is the law as at 2003.

ISBN: 0-595-32427-4 (pbk)
ISBN: 0-595-66572-1 (cloth)

Printed in the United States of America

Contents

Foreword

The author's sustaining interest in civil liberties permeates all her writings. This collection of human rights essays reveals the impact of the Human Rights Act 1998 on all aspects of British society. Topics covered include matters affecting asylum seekers, pornography, the right of a person in police custody to legal advice and the right to notify someone that he has been detained by the police, the legal right to protest in the United Kingdom, prisoners' rights, privacy and press freedom, as well as instances of the miscarriage of justice.

The comprehensive range and the author's acute insight into these everyday but essential legal issues in the United Kingdom make this book compulsory reading for any person wishing to have a full grasp of the legal scene in Britain today.

C H Muller, MA (Wales), PhD (Lond), DLitt (OFS), DEd (SA)

ESSAY 1: ASYLUM SEEKERS

Statutes

British Naturalization Act 1870

Aliens Act 1905

British Nationality Act 1981.

Asylum and Immigration Act 1999

Asylum and Immigration Act 1999.

Human Rights Act 1998.

Cases

R v Home Secretary ex parte Khawaja (1984) HL (E)

R v Home Secretary ex parte Bugdaycay (1987) HL (E)

R v Home Secretary ex parte SivaKumaran (1987) HL (E)

International Transport Roth GmbH v Home Secretary TLR 11/12/2001

Has Liberal British tradition always prided itself on having an "open door" policy regarding refugees, political asylum seekers and those who could demonstrate a claim to British Citizenship?

In "The Refugee in International Law", Guy Goodwin-Gill states the definition of refugees for the purposes of the United Nations. He says (page 7)...."The Office of the United Nations High Commissioner for Refugees (UNHCR) succeeded the IRO(International Refugee Organisation) as the principal UN agency concerned with refugees……. (page 17) the class of persons within the mandate of, or of concern to,UNHCR, includes (1) those who, having left their country, can, on a case-by-case basis, be determined to have a well-founded fear of persecution on certain specified grounds; and (2) those often large groups or categories or persons who, likewise having crossed an international frontier, can be determined or presumed to be without, or unable to avail themselves of, the protection of the government of their State of origin. This is the broad meaning of the term "refugee" for the purposes of the United Nations…

Britain's history is bound up with successive waves of refugees. Southampton, England, was one of the biggest in transmigration centres in the world at the turn of the 19th Century. In 1893 it was a stopping point for thousands of Jews fleeing pogroms in Russia and Eastern Europe. Most of the refugees went on to New York, but about 150,000 settled in the UK. The US sent the refugees back but Britain refused them.

(1) During the first world war, 250,000 Belgian refugees arrived in the UK in the biggest influx of the 20th Century.

(2) The British had pledged to defend Belgian neutrality and failed. Between 1939 and 1947 Britain accepted 130,000 Polish refugees. In 1944 Britain was one of the countries to allow Poland to fall into the Soviet sphere of influence. Then there was the arrival of the Ugandan Asians in 1970 and the Bosnians and Kosovans recently.

The harsh restrictions on immigration into the UK has not changed since the 1880's. when Jews immigrated to Britain. The Aliens Act 1905 restricted "undesirable and destitute immigrants", for example, people thought to be a charge on public funds or detriment to public health. In the first four years of the Act 1378 Jews were deported many of whom had lived with their families in Britain for years.

In the 1930's when another influx of Jews occurred the press and Trade Unions stirred up uneasiness among the population. In 1938, an editorial in the Sunday Express said…"but just now there is a big influx of foreign Jews into Britain. They are over-running the country. They are trying to enter the medical profession in great numbers. They wish to practice as dentists…".

By the start of the war about 55000 Jewish refugees came to Britain. Refuge to Britain was dependent upon the Jewish community providing for all of the refugees' needs until the government was forced into providing some assistance.(1a)

Recently, on the 2nd October 2000, there has been a change to citizenship legislation which began as long ago as 1377 with the dual-chamber parliament established under Edward the third. This change is the Human Rights Act and it is the second biggest change to the Justice system since the Magna Carta and gives the right to life and a fair trial, freedom from torture, freedom of expression and freedom to marry and have a family.

(3)This is a change to citizenship legislation which had began to take shape since the denotation of "British Citizenship" under the British Nationality Act 1981.

(4) Yet it is to be noted that, among the 26 EU member states, Britain still does not have an enforceable Bill of Rights

(5) In 1985, the governments of 5 EEC member states signed an agreement towards the "gradual abolition of checks at their common borders" in Schengen, a small town in Luxembourg. The UK did not sign this agreement. In 1995 a number of governments went ahead and put **the Schengen acquis** into force and in 1997 it was annexed to the Amsterdam Treaty by Protocol. Britain still has strong external border controls.

(6). In 2001 the question of strong internal control by way of national identity card is being debated.

(7). But Britain is not alone in this restrictive immigration policy. Restrictive immigration and asylum policies have been continually institutionalised from 1985 to 2000 by European "umbrella" agreements such as the "Schengen Accords", "the Dublin Convention", "the Third Pillar of the Maastricht Treaty" and "the Amsterdam Treaty".

(8). It seems that the European democracies, Britain included, nowadays limits universal liberal rights, as in the "1951 Geneva Convention Relating to Status of Refugees", to community, to protect its social and cultural integrity.

The free movement of people belongs among the basic human freedoms and liberties. The Article 13 of the "Universal Declaration of Human Rights "adapted by the UN in 1948 states

(3) Everyone has the right to freedom of movement and residence within the borders of each State and,
(a) Everyone has the right to leave any country, including his own, and to return to his country.

More specifically the 1951 Geneva Convention relating to the Status of Refugees secures for refugees "the widest possible exercise of…fundamental rights and freedoms". Article 1 refers to the term "refugee" as anybody who has "a well-founded fear of being persecuted for reason of race, religion, nationality, membership of a particular social group or political opinion". The Convention guarantees the right to asylum without conditions. In the summer of 2000 the British Home Secretary campaigned to overturn the Geneva Convention claiming that the Convention was outdated.

In 2000 Britain planned a new detention centre on the South coast which will be capable of holding several thousands of refugees awaiting processing.

In 2001 the British Government's immigration policy suffered a setback when the courts ruled that it was acting illegally in fining truck drivers £2000 for each stowaway brought to Britain. (12). Six conjoined applications for judicial review of decisions by the Secretary of State for the Home Department, namely that the six claimants were liable to penalties as persons responsible for clandestine entrants to the United Kingdom under the Immigration and Asylum Act 1999, The Carrier's Liability (Clandestine Entrants and Sale of Transporters) Regulations 2000 SI2000/658 and the Carrier's Liability (Clandestine Entrants) (Code of Practice) Order 2000 SI 2000/684. Evidence from the United Kingdom Immigration Service stated that the Act aimed to overcome the problems generated by the vast number of attempts to gain clandestine entry to the United Kingdom and to persuade lorry drivers to perform the necessary checks on their vehicles. The claimants were lorry drivers and/or owners or hirers of goods vehicles and trailers. They submitted in their application that the penalty regime introduced by the Act was a disproportionate response to the problem of clandestine entrants and the penalty regime was an unjustifiable restriction on the free movement of goods contrary to Article 28ECTreaty, failed to meet the procedural requirements of Article 6 European Convention on Human Rights. The government estimates that there are 400 to 800 illegal stowaways entering UK in this way each month and the fines regime was introduced in April 2000 under the Immigration and Asylum Act. It was held that the effect of the penalty regime amounted to violations of Article 28 and Article 49 EC Treaty that were not justifiable on public policy grounds because it did not comply with the Convention and was a disproportionate response to the problem of clandestine entry. Essentially this case is sited to illustrate the draconian measures the UK government will go to in order to quell its unjustified perception of an immigration problem.

Asylum in Britain today is very difficult to obtain.(13). The most recent asylum seekers in Britain are from Zimbabwe, Iran and Afghan. The Organisation Bail for Immigration Detainees tells of Zimbabweans put into detention and even maximum-security prisons whilst they await their hearings, even though some have relatives and friends here. To detain people on the basis of national identity is a breach of the European Convention

A look at the statistical facts on asylum seekers to the UK shows that from 1991 to 2000 there were between 15000 and 55000 asylum seekers a year. Appendix 2 shows total acceptances of all immigration for these years to be in the range of 50000 to 100000 a year. In these same years only 2000 to 10000 asylum seekers were granted settlement each year.

For example, looking at 1998, 6680 asylum seekers were granted settlement in a population of approximately 60 million people, that is, 0.01113 % of the

UK's population. This is by no means an significant proportion of the population and it is difficult to see any link between Britain's perception that it is asylum "friendly" and the statistical facts.

Conclusion

Britain subscribed to the European Declaration of Human Rights, adopted and proclaimed by the UN General Assembly's resolution in December 1948, and to the 1951 Geneva Convention Relating to the Status of Refugees. Britain's Home Secretary claimed that the agreement of the Convention was "outdated" and stated his intention to place the asylum law on a more rational basis, hence the Immigration and Asylum Act 1999.which imposes tight regulations on asylum (14). There is potential redress to asylum seekers already in the UK by way of the Human Rights Act 1998. If a public authority has acted in a way which is made unlawful by section 6 (1) of the Act, a person may bring proceedings against the authority under this Act in the appropriate Court or Tribunal if he or she is a victim of the unlawful act. Such remedies, however, need finances, which, often, genuine asylum seekers have none of.

The moral proclamations of liberalism in Britain have never really been borne out by liberal attitudes to refugees in reality in the past or in the present. The figures speak for themselves. The tight regulations in the Immigration and Asylum Act are contrary to Britain's own perception that it is a liberal country.

In the international picture, the UK was one of the first Western countries to legislate against immigration with the Naturalization Act 1870, applying constrains and restrictions on refugees, asylum seekers and those who wish to immigrate to a better life. [Appendix 5], although there is a Refugee Council in the UK which provides legal and other counselling as well as Human Rights Organisations (for example, Amnesty International) whose reporting,monitoring and lobbying activities include refugees and persecuted persons.

REFERENCES

1a. http://www.ujs-online.co.uk/magazine_place_home.htm.
1. Guardian Newspaper 23.05.2001.
"Haven't we been here before?"

2. Guardian Newspaper 04.12.2000
"Comment and Analysis": A.
4. "Civil Liberties & Human Rights in England & Wales &,D .Feldman (1993), Clarendon Press, Oxford.
5. "The Refugee in International Law", G.S.Goodwin-Gill, (1996),Clarendon Press, Oxford.
6. "Seizing the Middle Ground :Constructivism in World Politics" European Journal of International Relations .C. Adler(1997)
7. http://www.oneworld.org/index-oc/issue295/fisher.html
8. BBC News 12.2.2000 "Fresh row over asylum seekers
9. BBC News 18.4.2000. ""Asylum camp plan attacked".
10. http://wwww.parliament.the-stationery-office.co.uk
"Immigration Policy"
11. BBC News 18.4.2000."Asylum Camp plan attacked".
12. International Transport Roth GmbH v Home Secretary TLR 11/12/ 2001.
13. Guardian Newspaper 4.12.2001.
"Comment and Analysis: A safe haven, if convenient".
14. http://www.lawsociety.org.uk/dcs/fourth-tier.asp?section=893

STATUTES

British Naturalization Act 1870
Aliens Act 1905
British Nationality Act 1981.
Asylum and Immigration Act 1999
Asylum and Immigration Act 1999.
Human Rights Act 1998.

CASES

R v Home Secretary ex parte Khawaja (1984)HL(E)
R v Home Secretary ex parte Bugdaycay (1987)HL(E)
R v Home Secretary ex parte SivaKumaran (1987)HL(E)
International Transport Roth GmbH v Home Secretary TLR 11/12/2001

UK LEGISLATION among the INTERNATIONAL INSTRUMENTS on REFUGEES showing a restrictive trend.
British Naturalization Act 1870.
1905 UK Aliens Act *

1910   Brussels International Convention with respect to Assistance and Salvage at Sea.

1911   Arrangement with regard to the Issue of Identity Certificates to Russian Refugees.

1912   Arrangement relating to the Issue of Identity Certificates to Russian- and Armenian Refugees.

1913   Arrangement concerning the Legal Status of Russian and Armenian Refugees.

1914   Havana Convention on Asylum.

1915   Convention relating to the International Status of Refugees.

1916   Provisional Arrangement concerning the Status of Refugees coming from Germany.

1917   United Nations Charter.

1918   Universal Declaration of Human Rights.

1919   European Convention of Human Rights.

1920   Convention relating to the Status of Refugees.

1921   Geneva Convention *

1922   Caracas Convention on Diplomatic Asylum.

1923   European Convention on the Abolition of Visas for Refugees.

1924   Europea Agreement on Consular Functions & Protocol concerning Protection of Refugees.

1925   Protocol to the 1957 Agreement relating to Refugee Seamen.

1926   European Agreement on the Transfer of Responsibility for Refugees.

1927   Cartagena Declaration on Refugees.

1928   Afghanistan-Pakistan Agreement on Voluntary Return of Refugees.

1929   Convention on the Application of the Schengen Agreement.

1930   Treaty of Maastricht = EU Treaty

1996   UK Asylum and Immigration Act*.

1998   UK Human Rights Act

1999   UK Immigration and Asylum Act*

Appendix 5 constructed from pages xxiii to xxvii "The Refugee in International Law", G.S.Goodwin-Gill. and UK Butterworths search.

ESSAY 2: PORNOGRAPHY IN THE UNITED KINGDOM

Table of Cases

Calder & Boynes (1969) 1QB 151

DPP v Jordan (1976) 3 All ER 775

DPP v Whyte (1972) AC 849

Handyside v UK (1979-80) 1EHRR 737

Hicklin (1868) 3QB 360

Hoare v United Kingdom (1997) EHRLR 678

Moonen v Film and Literature Board (1999) NZAR324

Observer & Guardian v UK (1991) 14 EHRR 153

R v Anderson, R v Neville, R v Dennis, R v OZ Publications Ink Ltd (1972) 1QB 305

R v Video Appeals Committee of British Board of Film Classification ex parte British Board of Film Classification (2000) EMLR 850 (QBD)

R v Gibson and another (1990) CA

R v Perrin (2002) EWCA Crim 747

R v Farquhar (2002) EWCA Crim 1633

Table of UK and US Statutes

Broadcasting Act 1990

Cinemas Act 1985

Communications Decency Act 1996 (USA)

Investigatory Powers Act 2000

Human Rights Act 1998

Obscene Publications Act 1959

Theatres Act 1968

BRITISH PORNOGRAPHY

Introduction

Article 10 of the Human Rights Act 1998, "Freedom of expression", gives the right to give and receive information to and from each other, by guaranteeing the right to hold and express opinions and ideas. Journalists and publishers can use Article 10 to argue that there should be no restrictions on what they publish and writers and artists can use it to defend themselves against censorship and to argue for fewer restrictions on pornography.

Censorship of free expression can be reconciled by making it a criminal offence to commit obscene pornography through the medium of publication or broadcasting by deeming the display of pornography offensive, shocking and disturbing to any sector of society as qualified in Article 10(2).[1], assuming that society is characterised by pluralism, tolerance and broad-mindedness. It is of note that the wording of Article 10 Human Rights Act 1998 is the very same wording of Article 10 of the European Convention for the Protection of Human Rights and Fundamental Freedoms which was ratified by the United Kingdom in March 1951 and entered into force in September 1953. With this in mind, the cases such as **Handyside v UK**[2] and **Hoare v UK**[3] will be analysed and discussed in the light of the HRA 1998 to illustrate that the HRA 1998

---

1. Article 10(2) HRA'98 states: "The exercise of these freedoms, since it carries with it duties and responsibilities, may be subject to such formalities, conditions restrictions or penalties as are prescribed by law and are necessary in a democratic society, in the interests of national security, territorial integrity or public safety, for the prevention of disorder or crime, for the protection of health or morals, for the protection of the reputation or rights of others, for the preventing the disclosure of information received in confidence or for maintaining the authority and impartiality of the judiciary"
2. (1979-1980) 1EHRR 737
3. (1997) EHRLR 678 In the Hoare case the applicant sold pornographic videos by post. The videos showed anal intercourse, bondage and the consumption of feaces. He was charged with 6 counts of publishing obscene material and convicted and sent to jail for 2 1/2 years. He appealed to the European Court that this infringed his freedom of expression. He lost.

does not make much of an impact in the case of pornography, because the Obscene Publications Act still apparently holds strong, even though there is apparently a deluge of pornography in books, videos, magazines, billboards, etc. It is obvious that the context in which it is depicted and the degree of explicitness is important.

Pornography and the present relevant UK laws will be discussed—the Obscene Publications Act, Broadcasting Act, Cinemas Act. The issue of child pornography will be explored to illustrate that there must be a line drawn at freedom of expression, as qualified in Article 10(2) of the Human Rights Act. The Canadian and New Zealand treatment of this issue will be discussed and case law and relevant contemporary events will be considered side by side to show the contemporary social reality.

Censorship by way of Statutes

Censorship of free expression has always been(*see Appendix 1 on page 19*) and is still necessary as there is a need to maintain proper standards of taste and decency. The statutes of the Broadcasting Act 1990, Obscene Publications Act 1959 and the Cinemas Act 1985 are still in force, although the legislation today must be read by the courts in a manner which gives effect, as far as possible, to the European Convention on Human Rights as is stipulated in section 3 of the HRA 1998.

The Obscene Publications Act covers all media material. The Theatres Act covers live performances; the Broadcasting Act covers radio and television and the Cinemas Act covers cinemas.

The court's decision in the 1972 case of **Anderson** [4]would be different today. The courts would have to take into account contemporary standards of morality in applying the test of what is "to deprave and corrupt". The jury would have to ask first whether an article is obscene and pornographic, and, if so, to consider whether its merits outweigh its obscenity. This test is a means of giving protection to freedom of expression in relation to publications of artistic merit. Similarly, in **Gibson**[5], the merits of an obscene object would today prevent its suppression. This is borne out by art shows at present such as the Cuban sex video show[6] which was not prevented from being shown. Contrary

---

4. (1972)1QB 304
5. (1990)2QB 619,CA

to this libertarian attitude, publications such as magazines, some videos and some books can be and are seized today. The **Mapplethorpe** book is an example of this subjective and arbitrary reasoning. In this case the library of the University of Central England was raided by the West Midlands Police Paedophile and Pornography Squad who confiscated a book about Robert Mapplethorpe and his work because they declared parts of the book obscene. The case did not however get to court because the Crown Prosecution Service decided not to prosecute. It seems that the protection of HRA section 10 depends not only contextually, but also on the willingness of the prosecuting authorities to refrain from bringing prosecutions and also on the tolerance of magistrates, rather than on the law itself.

As far as broadcasting pornographic material is concerned, the Broadcasting Act only partly restrains freedom of expression. There is the Independent Television Commission which acts as a public body charged with licensing and regulating non-BBC television services and attempts to ensure that no programme offends against good taste and decency. It allows sexual scenes as long as they are presented with tact and discretion and so cannot be classed as pornography. In **R v Video Appeals Committee** [7] the Committee was overruled and seven pornographic videos were granted R18 classification. This shows the law being used in context of the present. social and moral climate of the UK. The case of **Rv Farquhar** also shows this change of tone in the law, acknowledging the moral climate today.

As far as films are concerned, it follows the guidelines laid down by the British Board of Film Classification and shows films containing sex only after a certain time (9PM) "watershed". The Broadcasting Standards Commission has the duty to create a Code of Guidance for broadcasts which deals with the depiction of sex (section 108 Broadcasting Act 1996). It can be said that these arrangements represent a slacking of restraints on what sex scenes can be broadcast.

---

6.   The Times Newspaper article 25/2/02: "Outrage at Cuban video sex show open to children" by Philip Pank…ten Cuban men are depicted from the waist down, bringing themselves to ejaculation. Children, accompanied by adults can view this film exhibition as long as the children are supervised…

7.   R v Video Appeals Committee (2002)EMLR 850 (QBD)

The Cinemas Act 1985 continues with an old power to censor the film industry.

To what extent the courts will provide a fair balance between freedom of expression via pornography and the protection of morality remains to be seen in caselaw.

There is no universal concept of morality[8] and what is pornography in one context may be classed as freedom of expression in another. The Handyside case shows that ECHR gave high value to public interest arguments in favour of publication. In this case the applicant was prosecuted under the Obscene Publication Acts 1959 and 1964 for having obscene books in his possession for gain. He had acquired the distribution rights for a publication called "The Little Red Schoolbook". This was an anti-authoritarian book aimed at teenagers which contained an explicit section on sexual activity.. The book was marketed as a schoolbook. He was fined £100 and the court ordered the seizure and destruction of his remaining stock. He appealed and the appeal was dismissed. He went to Strasbourg and complained that this was breaking Article 10 European Convention on Human Rights. It was found that the applicant's conviction was a breach of Article 10 ECHR, but it was held that as for Article 10(2) ECHR, the UK did interfere adequately as "prescribed by law" and held that the UK legislation of Obscene Publications Act pursued the legitimate aim of the protection of morals. The court stated this important principle :

"Freedom of expression constitutes one of the essential foundations of a democratic society, one of the basic conditions necessary for its progress and for the development of every man. Subject to paragraph 2 of Article 10, it is applicable not only to information and ideas that are favourably received, or regarded as inoffensive, but also to those that offend, shock, or disturb the state or any sector of the population. Such are the demands of that pluralism, tolerance and broadmindedness without which there is no 'democratic' society."

But still the court concluded that, having regard to the potential audience and the subject-matter of the book, it was within the UK's margin of appreciation to take criminal proceedings. This illustrates that material is defined as pornographic contextually. Today, because sexual material is the norm, apart from

---

8.   Handyside v UK (1979-80) 1 EHRR 737

hard pornography, the Crown Prosecution Service might have decided NOT to prosecute Handyside.. The Handyside case is similar in facts to the New Zealand case **Moonen v Film and Literature Board of Review** [9] The facts of this case were that the Customs and Excise submitted photos depicting children having sex. The Film and Literature Board classified them as objectionable under s3(2) of the 1993 New Zealand Obscene Publications Act. Moonen appealed on the grounds that this was a breach of his freedom of expression. The Board's decision was upheld, in a similar way as in the Handyside decision. So ten years later the mood as to the nature of pornographic and obscene seems not to have changed in the UK, Strasbourg, Canada and New Zealand. Yet it seems to be changing if we look at the cases of R v Video Appeals Committee and **R v Farquhar.**[10]

In the case of **The Observer & The Guardian v UK** [11] the ECHR considered that a strict test of necessity must be applied where the Government seeks to restrict journalistic freedom because it is in favour of the interest of democratic society in securing a free press. In general it seems today, that, if a broadcast containing pornography raises issues of public concern or public interest, then interference by the State or the courts is not justified. The Observer case shows that freedom of expression will be given greater guarantees in English courts in the future, although this seems to depend on the discretion of the government and the prosecuting authorities, rather than the law. The primacy of freedom of expression is to be restricted legitimately in the interest of public decency, the reputation of others, public morality, confidentiality and prevention of crime.

These legitimate restrictions have been around through censorship since the time of **Hicklin [1868]**[12].

---

9. Moonen v Film and Literature Board of Review (1999) NZAR 324 (HC(NZ)).
10. R v Farquhar (2002) EWCA Crim 1633. The defendant made an indecent video of children and was selling them. He received a jail sentence and appealed against it. The appeal was allowed to have the sentence greatly reduced.
11. Observer & Guardian v UK (1991) 14 EHRR 153.
12. Hicklin (1868) 3 QB 360.

As society develops, the meaning of words change. The 1959 Obscene Publications Act was passed in an attempt to clear up the uncertainty of what the term "to deprave and corrupt" means. The *actus reus* of the offence involves the publication of an article which tends to deprave and corrupt a significant proportion of those likely to see and hear it (section 1(1)). This is a crime of strict liability ; there is no need to show an intention to deprave and corrupt, merely an intention to publish.. Once it is shown that an article is obscene within the meaning of the Act, it is irrelevant if the defendant claims that his motive is pure and noble.[13] The obscenity or otherwise of material cannot be determined only be analysis of the material but by the character of the consumer exposed to it. In **DPP v Whyte** [14] the court looked at the type of shop and the class of person who goes there as well as the material itself. Lord Wilberforce said in summing up : "…and there is no basis for the argument that even if the effect was only on the mind and not directly on action, ie outside the Act,…influence on the mind is not merely within the law but it is its primary target…"

Today, the concept of obscenity is kept up to date in that the courts take account of changing standards of morality. That morality is changing is illustrated by new sex shops not only marketing for men but for women also. For example, there are sex shops in London named "Coco de Mer" and "Myla" for women.[15] Consider this event with the events in the **Gibson** case [16] where the defendants were convicted of the offence of displaying in an art gallery a model of a human head with earrings made out of freeze-dried human foetuses of three to four months gestation. At appeal it was argued that ""obscene" "could denote something which disgusted the public or had a tendency to corrupt". It was found that this was not so, but of artistic value. So society has been broadminded even before the Human Rights Act 1998. It seems that sex objects sold in sex shops do not upset the public; similarly, shows in art galler-

---

13. Calder and Boynes (1969) 1 QB 151.
14. DPP v Whyte (1972) AC 849. Mr & Mrs Whyte ran a bookshop and sold ordinary books as well as hard-core pornography. The case went to the House of Lords and the DPP were successful.
15. Guardian newspaper article 3/02/02 "They're having it all…really?" by Jocasta Shakespeare.
16. Gibson & Sylveire (1990) 2QB 619,CA.

ies do not really upset the public, however distasteful they may be to some of us.

As far as pornography is concerned section 3 of the Obscene Publications Act states that magazines and videos can be seized if they are obscene. This material is destroyed and no other punishment is imposed; so section 3 operates at a low level of visibility as no conviction is made and censorship is carried out by way of a seizure order.

In **DPP v Jordan** [17], the articles deemed obscene were hardcore pornography. The defendants tried to justify this pornography as being of psychotherapeutic value for persons of deviant sexuality and their defence was that the material might help to relieve sexual tensions by way of sexual fantasies. It was argued that such material might provide a safety value for such persons which would divert them from anti-social activities and that such benefit could fall within the words "other objects of general concern" deriving from section 4. But the House of Lords held that these words must be construed *ejusdem generis* with the preceding words "art, literature, learning, science". Today this might not be the case in the light of what is deemed art, literature, learning and science today.

Electronic Pornography

The onset of the computer age has its disadvantages as far as pornography is concerned.[18] A person can, in the privacy of his own home, download sexually explicit photographs if he or she wishes. The question of where to draw the line is the point at which his actions become unlawful. In the UK workplace it is not considered that viewing pornography at work-time on the internet is appropriate. Seventy two percent of UK firms have dealt with internet misuse and sixty nine percent of all dismissals were associated with on-line pornography. This is an example of pornography in context.[19] For example, it is a crime to create child pornography, send it to others or keep it in your own home.

---

17. DPP v Jordan (1977) AC 699
18. see R v Perrin (2002) EWCA Crim 747 A pornographic web site was set up outside the UK but was caught under the Obscene Publications Act s2(1) and s1(3).
19. New Law Journal 25/10/2002: "Cyber-risks—how are you managing them?"

The law defines children as any persons under the age of sixteen. Child pornography is illegal even if it may not be obscene because it is the sexual abuse of children and harms them. But although illegal, child pornography constitutes about seven percent of the pornography market.[20] So even if the making of it constitutes "freedom of expression", this is no mitigation for the crime of child pornography which "depraves and corrupts" as per the Obscene Publications Act. It can lure children into sexual activity and instruct them. Young children who view such material may be led to believe that this is acceptable behaviour.[21]

It cannot therefore be moral that persons wishing to exercise "freedom of expression" under the HRA can be allowed to make or publish such material because it takes away from the Human Rights of the children who are abused in the materials and from those of us who may view it unintentionally when such material is forced on us by way of the internet. This material may be legal in other countries from which it is sent, so our UK laws must censor and thus protect our community in the UK.

It may be to our benefit if the UK was to enact a Communications Decency Act as has the US[22] in their Communications Decency Act 1996 (CDA codified as 47U.S.S)[23]

Internet site providers are looking into filtering devices such as using an XXX top-level domain to provide adult-oriented only material with an easy way of recognising material inappropriate for children and discarding the need for a

---

20. "Child pornography on the internet" MG Water.
21. "Child sexual abuse: a handbook for health care legal professionals", by D. Schetsky & A Green, 1988, Brunner/Mazel Publishers, pp 154-157.
22. Journal IT Law Today: "US ISPS force new liability for child pornography"
23. US Communications Decency Act 1996 provides : whoever in intestate or foreign communications—makes, creates or solicits and initiates transmission of a comment, request, suggestion, proposal, image or other communication which is obscene or indecent, knowing that the recipient of the communication is under 18 years of age, regardless of whether the maker of such communication placed the call or intended the communication, shall be fined under the Title 18 United States Code, or imprisoned no more than two years or both.

laborious inspection of web pages for such content and simplifying the filtering task by blocking access to the sites in the XXX domain. But there still will be problems of age verification, for example, which can partly be countered by being fee-paying sites.

The Investigatory Powers Act 2000 which give the government routine powers to tap telephone calls can be used to open email messages. These essentially are to combat crime and is used to catch child pornography users. The government can now demand encryption keys to any and all data communications with a prison sentence of two years for those who do not comply. This may be seen as an invasion of privacy and a curtailment of a person's freedom of expression but is there to prevent harm to others. The internet, though, has always been censored, even before this further censorship, because, under the Obscene Communications Act as amended in 1994, computer disks are considered to fit the description of publishing under section 1(3) and the electronic transmission of pornographic material is covered.

Conclusion

The protection of morals requires a wide margin due to its subjective nature. Material can only be defined as pornographic contextually as there must remain a realm of private morality and immorality which is not the state's business. Nevertheless there needs to be law against harming others as is stipulated in the Human Rights Act Article 10(2) which qualifies the freedom of expression as per Article 10(1). This law need to be relevant to contemporary social reality. It also needs to be updated to keep up with obvious harmful criminal acts such as child pornography. It needs to keep up with the global electronic marketplace.

But howevermuch we respect the need for law and order, we have to admit that the law alone cannot enforce and censor moral standards for it can be argued that pornography is freedom of expression, freedom of sexual expression and it is only pornography in the context in which it is seen.
The social reality seems to be that to titillate the public with slight obscenity and provocative nudity is acceptable to the public and to the government and the degree of explicitness is gradually increasing. It is for the law to draw the line for the protection of the public and for the UK society to accept that it needs this protection.

Table of Cases

Calder & Boynes (1969)1QB 151
DPP v Jordan (1976)3 All ER 775
DPP v Whyte (1972) AC 849
Handyside v UK (1979-80) 1EHRR 737
Hicklin (1868) 3QB 360
Hoare v United Kingdom (1997) E.H.R.L.R. 678
Moonen v Film and Literature Board (1999)N.Z.A.R.324
Observer & Guardian v UK (1991) 14 EHRR 153
R v Anderson, R v Neville, R v Dennis, R v OZ Publications Ink Ltd (1972) 1QB 305
R v Video Appeals Committee of British Board of Film Classification ex parte British Board of Film Classification(2000) E.M.L.R. 850 (QBD)
R v Gibson and another (1990) CA
R v Perrin (2002) EWCA Crim 747
R v Farquhar (2002) EWCA Crim 1633

Table of UK and US Statutes

Broadcasting Act 1990
Cinemas Act 1985
Communications Decency Act 1996   [UNITES STATES]
Investigatory Powers Act 2000
Human Rights Act 1998
Obscene Publications Act 1959
Theatres Act

Bibliography
Books:

1. Butterworths Enclycopedia of Forms and Precedents:Entertainment and Media",2000.
2. Devlin.P, "The enforcement of morals", 1965, Oxford University Press
3. Outhwaite.W & Wheeler.M, "Guide to the Human Rights Act 1998", 2000, Old Bailey Press.
4. Cheney.D,Dickson.L,Fitzpatrick.J,Uglow.S., "Criminal Justice and the Human Rights Act 1998"1999, Jordans Publishers.
5. Feldman.D, "Civil Liberties and Human Rights in England and Wales",

1995, Oxford.University Press.
6. Fitzpatrick P & Hunt.A, "Critical Legal Studies", 1983, Blackwell Publishers.
7. Emerson.B & Ashworth.A, "Human Rights and Criminal Justice", 2001, Sweet & Maxwell Publishers.

Articles:

8. Shaw.S, "New Zealand : Freedom of expression—Censorship", 1999, Entertainment Law Review.
9. Edwards.S, "The Video Appeals Committee and the standard of legal Pornography", 2001, Criminal Law Review.
10. Cram.I, "Criminalising Child Pornography—A Canadian Study in Freedom of Expression and Charter-led Judicial Review of Legislative Policy-making", 2002,
Journal of Criminal Law.
11. New Law Journal 25/10/2002 "Cyber-risks—how are you managing them?"
Peter Hungerford-Welsh
12. Journal of Criminal Law 8/02 "Criminalising child pornography—a Canadian study in Freedom of expression & Charter-led Judicial Review of Legislative Policy-making", by Ian Cram
13. IT Law Today : "US ISPS force new liability for child pornography"

Internet web-sites

14. http://www.personal.umd
"Pornography and feminism"
15. http://www.legaltheory.demon.co.uk
"Real rapes"
16. http://www.isil.org
"Banning pornography endangers women"
17. http://www.joc.mit.edu
"Speaking out against the new prissiness"
18. http://www.ucalgary.ca
"Law and the feminist debate about pornography and censorship on the internet"
19. http://www.spectacle.org
"Pornography is Oppression"

20. http://www.nesli.ac.uk
"The harms of sex and the risks of breasts: obscenity in Canadian Law"
21. http://www.nesli.ac.uk
"Prosecuting 'Child Pornography': Possession and taking of photographs of children"
22. http://www.humanrights.org.uk
"Human Rights update from One Crown Office Row"

Newspaper Articles:

23. Guardian 3/02/02 "They're having it all...really?" by Jocasta Shakespeare.
24. Guardian 21/02/02 "Microsoft is the new porn" by Bobbie Johnson.
25. The Sunday Times 24/02/02 "The future looks blue as mobile firms turn to sex" by Paul Durham.
26. The Times 25/02/02 "Outrage at Cuban video sex show open to children" by Philip Pank.

Appendix

STATUTES AND CONVENTIONS THAT HAVE PROTECTED THE UK PUBLIC AGAINST PORNOGRAPHY THROUGH TIME

1876	CUSTOMS CONSOLIDATION ACT	UK
1950	European Convention on Human Rights	EU
1952	Customs and Excise Act	UK
1953	Post Office Act	UK
1955	Children and Young Persons (Harmful Publications)Act	UK
1956	Sexual Offences Act	UK
1959	Obscene Publications Act	UK
1968	Trade Descriptions Act	UK
1968	Theatres Act	UK

1971	Unsolicited Goods and Services Act	UK
1978	Protection of Children Act	UK
1981	Indecent Displays (Control) Act	UK
1984	Data Protection Act	UK
1984	Video Recordings Act	UK
1985	Interception of Communications Act	UK
1990	Broadcasting Act	UK
1993	Sexual Offences Act	UK
1998	Human Rights Act	UK
2000	ELECTRONIC COMMUNICATIONS ACT	UK
2000	Regulation of Investigatory Powers Act	UK

ESSAY 3: THE UK'S POLICE AND CRIMINAL EVIDENCE ACT AND THE ARRESTED SUSPECT

THE UK'S POLICE AND CRIMINAL EVIDENCE ACT AND THE ARRESTED SUSPECT

The Police and Criminal Evidence Act 1984 came into force on 1st January, 1986.

Essentially, a suspect in police custody has the right to legal advice, the right to notify someone that he has been detained by the police and the right to read the Codes of Practice governing his detention.

Section 58 PACE 1984 states that an arrested suspect is entitled to consult a solicitor of his choice and obtain legal advice. The police are not allowed to delay the suspect's request to access to a solicitor except in cases where the detainee is being held for a serious arrestable offence or an officer of at least superintendent has authorised the delay because there are reasonable grounds for believing that legal advice would lead to interference with evidence of an offence or hinder the recovery of the proceeds of an offence.(1)

Case law and research findings show that most suspects are not made truly aware of their rights and are often interviewed by very junior police officers and are very rarely given the Codes of Practice to read. The police are not allowed to delay acting on such a request, yet in practice it happens. Recent case law decisions McGuiness[1999]CLR 318 and Ionnu[1999] CLR 586 are cases where inference was taken on exercise of the right to silence.

Section 37(1) PACE 1984 states…"..The custody officer………shall determine whether he has before him sufficient evidence to charge a person with the offence for which he was arrested and may detain him at the police station for such period as necessary to enable him to do so." Further interview and further detention would be unlawful.(2).

If the custody officer believes there is sufficient evidence to charge, the suspect must be charged (or released). The custody officer must make a subjective decision. If the suspect wishes to terminate the interview by saying nothing more, it must be terminated. thus forcing the officer to make a decision.

On the day that the Birmingham Six had their convictions quashed, the Prime Minister announced the establishment of the Royal Commission on Criminal Justice and the right to silence was specifically a subject to be addressed. In December 1993 there was a Criminal Justice and Public Order Bill to abolish the right to silence.(20).

The right to silence is linked to arrested suspects having or not having legal advice in Police stations. In an ACPO 1993 study, 57% of suspects who had legal advice exercised their right to silence compared with 13% of those who did not have legal advice. This is corroborated with the research by the Royal Commission on Criminal Justice. (Appendix 2)

The reality is that there is no right to silence ; the Police do deny the suspect legal advice for up to thirty six hours if they think fit and they do detain suspects for as long as five days without charge instead of the mandatory six hours.

Section 58 PACE 1984 gives effect to the rights of suspects to legal advice. Section 59 PACE provides for an organised and coordinated scheme of defence advice, free at the point of delivery. Yet the Annual Report 1994 of the Legal Aid Board notes that only some 30% of arrested suspects have legal advice in the Police station either in person or over the telephone. Why only 30% of arrested suspects have legal advice begs the question as to whether all are told of this right. Yet in some cases, evidence obtained in breach of PACE is sometimes admitted at trial. The rights of the suspect and his protection by a defence lawyer is desirable in securing reliable confession evidence.(21)..

The reality is that PACE 1984 does not protect those who are arrested without warrant by the Immigration and Asylum Act 1999 or the Prevention of Terrorism Act 1989 or the Terrorism Act 2000.

In Hough v Chief Constable of Staffordshire CA TLR 14.2.2001.} (3). The decision in Hough is contrary to the decision in Julie Ann Clarke v Chief Constable of North Wales Police CA 22.5.2000.Lawtel. (4).In the Julie Ann Clarke case there was no case found for wrongful arrest. Wrongful arrest cases abound.

A case where a person incriminated himself in conversation prior to arrest and caution is Rv Wayne Blackford CA 21.2.2000 Lawtel.(5)and this was admissable is in contrast to the decision in R v Glen Michael Wyna CA 27.4.2000 Lawtel in which such an interview was deemed a breach of PACE and Police Codes of Practice.(6).

Section 117 PACE 1984 states..."Where any provision of this Act—

a.   confers a power on a constable, and

b.   does not provide that the power may only be exercised with the consent of some person, other than a Police officer, the officer may use reasonable force, if necessary, in the exercise of power. But in R v Jones, R v Nelson CA TLR21.4.99. it is clear that reasonable force cannot be used to effect a confrontation as a means of identification of a suspect by a witness.(7)

The case of R v Anthony Leroy Forbes HL TLR 19.12.2000.,(8) on the other hand was of a failure to hold an identification parade in breach of Code D:2.3Code of Practice and Section 78 PACE 1984, as was also found in another successful appeal R v Nigel Nunes CA 31.10.2001 Lawtel.(9).

PACE 1984 defines "arrestable" offences as being those carrying possible prison sentences of five years or more except in the cases of sexual offences, Her Majesty's Customs crimes, property crimes, conspiring to commit an arrestable offence and offences under the Official Secrets Act.(10).

There is no specific rule as to how long a person may be detained before appearing before a Magistrate's Court. There is only common reasonable practice, the Phillips recommendation and guidelines.

Cases abound of offences treated contrary to PACE 1984,some very trivial.. One such case is Abdul Ghafar v Chief Constable of West Midlands Police (2000) CA 12.5.2000 extempore Lawtel in which a man was arrested for not wearing a seat-belt in a car, was awarded damages for wrongful imprisonment but an appeal was upheld. (11)..

In a contrasting decision in, Ronald Wilson v Chief Constable of Lancashire Constabulary CA 23.11.2000 Lawtel (12),Wilson was arrested for stealing a cheque and cashing it and it was found to be an unlawful arrest as the arrest did not comply with Section 28 PACE 1984.

Section 55 (1) PACE 1984 governs intimate body searches of arrested suspects. Section 55(1) PACE 1984 states....
"subject to the following provisions of this section, if an officer of at least the rank of *superintendent* has reasonable grounds...(13)

Yet it is often (14) the lower grade constables who conduct arrests, interviews and make decisions as to whether arrested suspects should be examined, personally searched, etc., even in serious cases.

Section 55 (1)(b) PACE 1984 states that searches must be carried by a "suitably qualified person (a medical practitioner or registered nurses).But often searches are carried out by the Police officers themselves.

When DNA samples are taken, under PACE 1984, they must be destroyed if the suspect is acquitted or the charge discontinued. (15) But this is not the case.

In the case R v Joe Smith CA TLR 20.12.2000.(16) the removal of non-intimate samples for DNA profiles was found not to be in breach of the European Human Rights Convention..

Apart from the powers in PACE 1984, the Police have further powers under the Criminal Justice and Public Order Act 1994 with respect to stop and search (17), search and seizure, power of arrest and detention.(18).

The Police have to make difficult decisions, subject to challenge by the Courts, on, for example, excluding a solicitor from an interview in the Police station, or whether a particular arrested suspect should be further detained when the clock under PACE is running.(19). Appendix 1 supports this. (14).

The Royal Commission on Criminal Justice in its report "Safeguards of suspects"(1993) considered ways of imposing implementation of PACE and Police Code C but declared itself satisfied that their provisions are generally accepted and complied with.. Appendix 2 shows the Royal Commission's findings (22), that the Police carry out significant interviews outside the Police station.[(23) and (24) R v Alexander Francis Allen and R v Stratford Youth Court,& N.Harding,etc. ex parte DPP)].

The Royal Commision's Report on Standards of supervision of Police Officers who interview suspects show that the majority of interviewing Police lack training and are of the lower ranks,even in serious cases.(14)

CONCLUSION

The ultimate protection for the rights of the arrested suspect would be judicial review. (25).
IN the law of arrest and search, the wide rules of judicial review which have evolved over many years as a means of ensuring that administrators and others act within the four corners of their authority give the ultimate protection for the rights of the arrested person.There are many challenges based on the ultra vires rule in response to PACE and are a useful reminder of the difficulties of statutory interpretation which underline so much of administrative law.Allegations of uncertainty can and do succeed.(9).

There is strong ground for reinforcing traditional common law presumptions in favour of personal freedom.

In the case of public interest immunity, the Crown or the Police seek to withold, on the grounds of public interest, the production of documentary or other evidence in a court of law.

The importance of notice has been widely recognised as an important ingredient of the right to be heard under the implied rules of natural justice

References

1.   http://www.startlawmachine.com/engwls/uklic
     "Police Powers".

2.   http://www.macdonald.butterworths.co.uk.
     "No comment, no inference."

3.   Hough v Chief Constable of Staffordshire CA TLR 14.2.2001.
     When the grounds for an arrest were based on an entry on the Police National Computer, the test of reasonableness should be applied to the

officer making the arrest and not to the officer who put the information into the computer. On 22nd June 2000, Hough was arrested, assaulted and imprisoned. He was a front-seat passenger in a car stopped by the Police on the motorway for having a damaged windscreen. A Mr. Skeldon owned the car. The Police National Computer entry read that the occupants of the car could be armed with a firearm. No firearms were found. Mr. Hough claimed damages.

4.   Julie Ann Clarke v Chief Constable of North Wales Police CA 22.5.2000 Lawtel.
Initial suspicion rested on three people. It was appropriate to hold all three until they were interviewed before deciding whether there was enough evidence to warrant a charge against any of them. It was wrong to adopt an over-lawyerly approach which required an officer to refer to the class of the drug on arrest because they had no power to arrest in relation to a class C drug.

5.   R v Wayne Blackford CA 21.2.2000.Lawtel.
In an unsuccessful appeal against conviction for an offence of handling stolen goods, a conversation between the Police and the appellant prior to his arrest and caution was admissable because the Police had questioned him only on "information received" about which nothing was known.

6.   R v Glen Michael Wyna CA 27.4.2000 Lawtel.
Questions asked by Police at the roadside, when there had been sufficient information to reasonably suspect the accused of an arrestable offence, constituted an interview, and without a caution and contemporary notes, was in breach of the Codes of Practice c:10.1, C:11.1A, C:11.5, C:11.7, C:11.10 and C:11.2A. and the Police's evidence of questions and answers at the roadside should have been excluded under Section 78 PACE 1984.

7.   http://www.psds.co.uk
"Can reasonable force be used to effect confrontation?"by J.Bird (Simon Muirhead & Burton).

8.   R v Anthony Leroy Forbes HL TLR 19.12.2000.
Code D:2.3 Code of Practice in circumstances where identification parades were to be held was clear if
a) the Police had sufficient information to justify the arrest of a particular

person for suspected involvement of an offence and

b) an eye witness had identified or might be able to identify that person and

c) the suspect disputed his identification

then an identification parade must be held if

a) the suspect consented and

b) paragraph 2:4, 2:7, 2:10 of Code D Police Code of Practice did not apply. In this case the Court of Appeal decided contrary to its own earlier decision in R v Popat (1998) 2 CAR 208.

9. R v Nigel Nunes CA 31.10.2001. Lawtel.
   In a successful appeal against conviction, the identification evidence of a Police officer breached Paragraph D:2.1 of the Code of Practice D. issued under the Police and Criminal Evidence Act 1984. Nunes submitted that, in the light of the decision in R v Forbes (2001) 2WLR 1, both the failure to hold an identification parade and the way in which the Police officer identified Nunes breached Code of Practice D. The conviction was unsafe and set aside.

10. http://www.magnacartaplus.orgs/bills/civ-lib
    "Police and Criminal Evidence Act 1984 (summary)".

11. Abdul Ghafar v Chief Constable of West Midlands Police CA 22.5.2000.Lawtel.
    The defendant Abdul Ghafar was arrested after he was stopped for not wearing a seat-belt.
    Section 28 PACE 1984 required a Police officer to advise an arrested person both of grounds of arrest and the specific general arrest condition that the officer intended to rely upon.
    The recorder was wrong in law to have concluded that a Police officer had to demonstrate a causal link between two issues and accordingly the arrest was not unlawful.

12. Ronald Wilson v Chief Constable of Lancashire Constabulary CA 23.11.2000. Lawtel.
    Where facts were known to the Police and could have been made known to arresting officers, it was unfair to arrest a suspect for an unidentified offence that took place at some unspecified time and place. Such an arrest was unlawful contrary to s 28(3)PACE 1984.

Wilson was arrested on 5.11.1996 on suspicion of theft, for which no criminal proceedings were ever brought. The complainant had had cheques stolen out of his cheque book,one of which was cashed in a bank. The complainant had supervised Wilson on a course at the premises from which the cheques were stolen and recognised Wilson on a video from the bank at the relevant time. Wilson said he had gone to the bank to change some money but did not consider that relevant to tell the arresting officer and was only told he was being arrested for theft, not the specific theft of a cheque.

13. http://www.bma.org.uk.
    "Guidelines for doctors asked to perform intimate body searches".

14. "The Royal Commission on Criminal Justice—Conduct of Police Investigations, Records of Interview, Defence of Lawyer's Role, Standards of Supervision. Research Studies No. 2, 3 & 4." HMSO 1994 ISBN 0 11 341050 6.

15. http://news.bbc.co.uk
    BBC News "A catalogue of criminals".

16. R v Joe Smith CA TLR 20.12.2000.
    There was no principle in English law that information received by a judge during a public interest immunity investigation could not be used by him to determine whether the Police has reasonable suspicion that a defendant had committed an offence or had reasonable cause to arrest him. That procedure did not constitute a violation of the defendant's rights enshrined in Article 6 European Convention on Human Rights. The Defendant was appealing against conviction for burglary. Blood was found on an article stolen. The Defendant was arrested and a hair sample taken from him without his consent.

17. http://www.bmf.co.uk
    "Briefing on the implications of the Criminal Justice and Public Order Act for motorcyclists".

18. PACE UPDATE
    Solicitors Journal SJ Vol 144 No. 18 Pages 441-442.

19. "The criminal process—an evaluative study", Andrew Ashworth, 1995, Clarendon Press, Oxford.

20. "Suspicion and Silence—The Right to Silence in Criminal Investigations" David Morgan & Geoffrey Stephenson (1994), Blackstone Press, ISBN 1 85431 380 0.

21. "Justice and efficiency? The Royal Commission on Criminal Justice", Stewart Field & Philip A.Thomas, 1994, Blackstone Publishers, ISBN 0 631 19348 0.

22. "The Royal Commission on Criminal Justice—Questioning & Interviewing of suspects outside Police Stations. Research Study No.22" 1993, HMSO ISBN 0 11 341085 9.

23. R v Alexander Francis Allen CA 25.7.2001 Lawtel.
Significant and substantial breaches of the PACE 1984 were likely to lead to the exercise of the Court's discretion to exclude evidence under Section 78 PACE, in particular where an admission or confession had been obtained after such breaches.
This was an appeal against conviction of robbery on 21.6.91. of the contents of a mailbag snatched by three men. The Defendant was arrested and there was a purported cell conversation, but the postman's description of the attacker was entirely unlike the defendant. The conviction was held to be unsafe.

24. R v Stratford Youth Court & n.Harding, M.Oshin ex parte DPP. DC 26.7.2001. Lawtel extempore.
A case where a judge had excluded evidence of an interview with a 17 year old suspect for breaches of Section 76 and 78 PACE 1984 was remitted to the youth Court for submission on whether the failure to provide an appropriate adult breaches Police Code of Practice C. It was alleged that the three had mugged a young man and stolen his mobile phone.

25. "Criminal law—Essays in honour of JC SMITH" 1987 Pages 170-180, Butterworths ISBN 0 406 501106.

ESSAY 4: THE EROSION OF THE POWER TO PROTEST IN THE UNITED KINGDOM

Table of Cases

posters and stickers were displayed in public places in the area. Muslims attending the mosque were subject to verbal abuse, threats of violence and sporadic attacks. The Crown Prosecution Service did not prosecute because it decided, that as section 17 of the Public Order Act 1986 defined "racial hatred" as "hatred against a group of persons in Great Britain defined by reference to colour, race, nationality or ethnic origins" that Muslims as a group were not covered by section 17 of the Act. It was held that a declaration that Muslims were a group covered by sections 17 and 19 of the Act would not be binding on the Criminal Court.

There are also offences of conspiracy to corrupt public morals and conspiracy to outrage public decency.
Even the laws on censorship affect power to protest. Theatres are subject to the laws on obscenity, defamation and incitement to racial hatred. Cinemas are licenced by the local authority which attaches conditional recommendations of the British Board of Film Censor.

The Police al Evidence Act 1984 and the Public Order Act 1986 confer on the Police significant powers with regard to freedom of movement and expression. The former allows the use of road blocks and searches as a measure, whilst the latter reforms and codifies public order laws, imposing more coherent powers for the policing of demonstrations, processions and assemblies. Coupled with these measures are the requirements in most circumstances for the due authorization to organise these activities.

Legislation and its Interpretation

The Terrorism Act 2000 gives rise to the Prevention of the full exercise of certain public rights. Before this time, the free movement and free expression of persons in airport premises was restricted by the imposition of imprisonable sanctions for those who enter aircraft without authorization or make misleading statements about the contents of luggage
The primary use of the law is to protect society
The Emergency Powers Act was used five times in the 1970's by the Conservative Government.

In March 2001 the Labour Government banned 21 groups, the majority Islamic, which it had branded as terrorist, enabling it for the first time to proscribe organisations targeting foreign states.

Section 1 of the Terrorism Act states:

1 (1) In this Act "terrorism" means the use or threat of action where—

(a) the action falls within subsection (2)

(b) the use or threat is designed to influence the government or to intimidate the public

or a section of the public, and

(c) the use or threat is made for the purpose of advancing a political, religious or ideological cause.

1 (2) Action falls within this subsection if it—

(a) involves serious violence against a person

(b) involves serious damage to property

(c) endangers a person's life, other than that of the person committing the action

(d) creates a serious risk to the health or safety of the public or a section of the public or

(e) is designed seriously to interfere with or seriously disrupt an electronic system.

1(3) The use or threat of action falling within subsection (2) which involves the use of firearms or explosives is terrorism whether or no9t subsection (1)(b) is satisfied.

Nearly all protest action would fulfil one of these objectives, or could be argued to, and therefore this condition could be easily satisfied. Section (2)(b) could be used against direct action protests such as road protests.. Section (2)(e) can be used against protests such as e-mail lobbying or client-side denial-of-service actions. Any kind of protest action on the Internet where people send information to a particular location, is bound to cause congestion and would meet the condition in subsection (2)(e). This Terrorism Act enables the investigation of persons, which can be disruptive to their campaigning activities.

But there is a general requirement that officers investigating terrorism must act in accordance with relevant codes of practice, ie. PACE Code of Practice and National Criminal Intelligence Service Code of practice. officers are required to work in accordance with the Codes but, under the Act, breaches of the Codes do not make officers liable for criminal or civil proceedings but can be used as evidence in criminal proceedings. The Act gives powers of search and arrest and detention and the ability to detain for 48 hours without access to legal assistance.

In November 2001 the Labour Government announced a new terrorism bill with added internment for any foreigners suspected of being terrorists. There are mechanisms for the Home Secretary to add other organisations to the list.

The Terrorism Act makes provision for the investigation of "terrorism". Section 1'(1) and 1 (2) of the Act can mean that protest groups can be caught in this definition. Subsec5tion 1(b) states…"…the use or threat is designed to influence the government OR to intimidate the public or a section of the public." The use of the word OR in this context means that the items in the S1(2) list can be interpreted separately, in order to satisfy the condition. The use of the word OR means one of the interpretations of what constitutes terrorism would be an action that is designed to influence the government. Nearly all protest action would fulfil one of these objectives or could be argued to do so.

CASE LAW DEVELOPMENTS

In the case R V Chief Constable of Devon & Cornwall, ex prate Central Electricity Generating Board (1981) 3 All ER 826 [1982] QB 458, the CEGB applied mandamus, directing Chief Constables to instruct Police to remove or assist Cab's servants/agents to remove protesters obstructing a survey being made by CEGB under statutory powers. It was held that the case was not one for mandamus. The protesters' actions were unlawful (s281 (2) Town and Country Planning Act 1971) and amounted to criminal conspiracy. The Cab's servants/agents were entitled to remove protesters and manhandle them provided that force was limited to the minimum necessary.

There was no need for the Police to intervene as long as the protesters did not resist being removed although Police constables have the duty to preserve the peace. But Police are not without powers as to passive resistors on private land. If the obstructers were 3 or more in number and by their conduct showed an intention to use violence to achieve their aims or otherwise behaved in a tumultuous manner, any constables present had the duty to disperse them because the protesters would then be guilty of unlawful assembly.

The case of <u>Monsanto</u> <u>Plc</u> <u>V</u> <u>Rowan</u> <u>Tally</u> <u>&</u> <u>ors</u> <u>(1999)</u> <u>CA</u> is a case of trespass to land and trespass top goods in which the respondents, in a claim for an injunction to restrain the destruction of Monsanto's genetically modified crops, did NOT have an arguable defence to a claim in trespass in land and goods, on the ground that their actions were justified as being necessary to protect third parties or in the public interest The defendants had destroyed Monsanto's genetically modified trial crop.

The unreported case of <u>Department</u> <u>of</u> <u>Trade</u> <u>&</u> <u>ors</u> <u>V</u> <u>Williams</u> <u>&</u> <u>74</u> <u>ors</u> <u>(1995)</u> <u>QBD</u> shows that matters can be taken a few stages further when protesters defied injunctions and the DTI claimed damages from the 75 protesters who tried to prevent them from building the M3 Motorway. The plaintiff acceded because the protesters did not have the means to satisfy any judgements to be made. Judge Allot ordered the defendants to make a contribution of £500 each to the costs of the plaintiffs, the substantial balance borne by the taxpayer.

Note that in this case injunctions were granted to the DTI to keep the trespassing protesters off their land, protesters being individually named. Yet in the case <u>Huntingdon</u> <u>Life</u> <u>Sciences</u> <u>Plc</u> <u>V</u> <u>John</u> <u>Curtin</u> <u>&</u> <u>ors</u> <u>(1998)</u> <u>CA</u>, an appeal against a refusal to grant an ex prate injunction to prevent harassment to the plaintiff company was held. An ex prate injunction would be inappropriate in this case because of the problems of identifying the defendants as some of the defendants had no legal personality.
In the case <u>London</u> <u>Animal</u> <u>Rights</u> <u>News</u> <u>V</u> <u>Peat</u> <u>Animal</u> <u>Action</u> <u>(1998)</u>CA an appeal =against a refusal to grant an ex prate injunction to prevent harassment to the plaintiff company was held. An ex-prate injunction would be inappropriate in this case because of problems of identifying the defendants as some had no legal personality.

In
<u>R</u> <u>V</u> <u>Coventry</u> <u>Airport,</u> <u>R</u> <u>V</u> <u>Dover</u> <u>Harbour</u> <u>Board,</u> <u>R</u> <u>V</u> <u>Associated</u> <u>British</u> <u>P</u> <u>orts</u> <u>(1995</u> <u>3</u> <u>All</u> <u>ER</u> <u>37</u>, bans on export livestock induced by unlawful acts of

animal rights protesters were held to be unlawful. These were applications for judicial reviews of decisions by respondent authorities to ban the export of live animals because of disruption by animal rights protesters. It was held that the export of live animals for slaughter though regarded by many as immoral, was lawful. The violent conduct of protesters was unlawful. It disrupted the rights of others to go about their lawful business. Applications against Coventry and Dover were allowed.

The case R V Chief Constable of Sussex, ex prate International Trader's Ferry Ltd (1999) HL, went a stage further in that animal protesters had the right to peaceful demonstration which impeded the delivery of livestock to Shoreham Harbour but the Police refused to provide full cover to protect lorries from animal protesters. The Police agreed to provide presence for two days a week only. The Chief Constable appealed the decision which upheld the applicant's challenge to the Chief Constable's refusal to extend Police protection against animal rights protesters on all working days.

It was held Article 34.1 EC Treaty provides that quantitative restrictions on exports and all measures having equivalent effect shall be prohibited by Member States. The Chief Constable's actions amounted to a prima facie breach of Article 34.. Had the Chief Constable decided on part-time protection for domestic purposes, it might have been deemed to be a reasonable decision. Here the EU law gives Police more power to curb protesters than in the Huntingdon case or the the CEGB case.

Protesters, on the other hand, have tried to use Articles 10 and 11 of the European Convention on Human Rights to defend their conduct and assert that they are exercising the rights of free speech and association. and or—

In the case of Silverton s V Zilberkweit and ors (2001) QBD (unreported) the 2nd and 3rd claimants were directors of the 5th claimant company which retailed furs. The 1st and 4th claimants were the spouses of the 2nd and 3rd claimants. The claimants applied for injunctions restraining the defendants from harassing the claimants under the Protection from Harassment Act 1997. They claimed that they had been harassed by animal rights activists at the company's shop and at their homes. An interim injunction was made and they sought to make it permanent. It was held that the court also imposed an exclusion zone in the permanent injunction, this zone being the street in which the fur shop was situated. This case shows the draconian might of the court in granting a permanent injunction against the protesters and puts a stop to this particular protest for all time. This can be seen in the light that the court has granted an injunction to protect commercial interests. balancing against the public right to information against private profit and ensuring that a debate is prevented.

What is the consequence of protesting after such an injunction is granted? In the case DPP V Joanna Moseley & ors (1999) DC, the respondents were acquitted of charges contrary to s2 Protection from Harassment Act 1997. The respondents were protesters at a licensed mink farm which was in keeping with the Mink (Keeping) (Amendment) Regulations 1997. The mink farmers obtained an injunction preventing persons from entering the farm or land close by. However further protests took a course of conduct amounting to harassment between 20th July 1997 and 19th March 1998. The respondents claimed that the conduct was reasonable. It was held that an injunction had to be obeyed unless and until it was varied and or set aside. Therefore the 3rd defendant (named in the injunction) was found guilty.

CONCLUSION

Despite the Human Rights Act there is an alarming erosion of civil liberties. The recent Criminal Justice Act removes the right to silence and restricts many kinds of peaceful protest. These measures have removed long established rights. The right to protest is a vital feature of democracy

Table of Cases

1. R V Gaunt (1948)

2. R V Arrowsmith [1975] QB678

3. Jordan V Burgoyne [1963] 2QB744

4. 4 Mandla V Dowell Lee [1983] 2AC548

5. Chandler V DPP [1964] AC763

6. R V Chief Constable of Devon & Cornwall (1982) QB458

7. Department of Trade V Williams & 74 ors (1995) QBD

8. R V Coventry Airport (1995) 3All ER37

Table of Statutes

14. Terrorism Act 2000

15. Investigatory Powers Act 2000.

16. Prevention of Terrorism Act 1996.

Bibliography

1. "The International Law of Human Rights", P.Seighart(1984) Oxford Univ. Press

2. "The EU and Human Rights",P.Alston (1999) Oxford Univ.Press

3. "The European Convention on Human Rights" F.G.Jacobs & R.C.A White (1996) Oxford University Press

4. "International Human Rights in context" H.J.Steiner & P.Alston (1996) Oxford University Press

5. "Civil Liberties and Human Rights in England and Wales" D.Feldman (1993)Oxford University Press

6. http://guardian.co.uk/humanrights/story/0,7369,444649,00.html "21 groups banned under new terror law"

7. http://www.observer.co.uk/comment/story/0,6903,480107,00.html "Power to the people"

8. http://www.schnews.org.uk/index.html "Blunkett ban"

9. http://content.techweb.com/wire/story/TWB19990726S0010 "UK faces protest over E-Commerce Bill"

10. http://www.observer.co.uk/libertywatch/story/0,1373,561488,00html ""Are civil liberties at risk? Yes, says Bill Morris"

11. http://www.observer.co.uk/libertywatch/story/0,1373,560757,00html "More democracy, more security"
Bibliography and References (continued).......

12. http://www.observer.co.uk/libertywatch/story/0,1373,564634,00.html
    "Now we really need rights"

13. http://www.jb.mam.ac.uk/~amsr/libscitech.html
    "A festival of rights"

14. http://www.libparty.demon.co.uk/ge97/civlibs.htm
    "Civil liberties"

15. http://www.gn.apc.org/action/csir/ta-brief.html
    "The terrorism Act 2000"

16. http://www.historylearningsite.co.uk/citizenship2.htm
    "What is citizenship?"

ESSAY 5: THE MAGUIRE CASE—A FAMOUS MISCARRIAGE OF JUSTICE THAT CHANGED THE FACE OF UK LEGISLATION

Table of Cases

Brogan v UK A/145-B, 11EHRR 117 (1988)

Ireland v UK A25 (1978)

R v Maguire and others (1991) CA

Ramdeen v State of Trinidad & Tobago, (1999) Privy Council.

R v Keane (1994) WLR 746

R v Selvage (1982) QB 372

R v Silverlock [1894] 2Qb 766

R v Rowell (1978) 1WLR 132

Table of Statutes

Administration of Justice (Miscellaneous Provisions) Act 1933.

Administration of Justice Act 1996.

Criminal Appeal Act 1995.

Criminal Evidence Act 1898.

Criminal Evidence Act 1968.

Criminal Justice Act 1987.

Criminal Justice Act 1988.

Criminal Justice Act 1991.

Criminal Justice and Police Act 2001.

Criminal Justice and Public Order Act 1994.

Criminal Law Act 1967.

Criminal Law Act 1977.

Criminal Procedure Act 1865.

Criminal Procedure and Investigations Act 1996.

The European Convention on Human Rights

Interception of Communications Act 1985

Human Rights Act 1998..

Magistrates Courts Act 1980.

Magistrates Courts (Advance Notice of Expert Evidence) Rules 1997

Northern Ireland (Emergency Provisions) Act 1973.

Official Secrets Act 1989

Police and Criminal Evidence Act 1984.

Prevention of Violence (Temporary Provisions) Act 1939.

Public Order Act 1936.

Terrorism Act 2000.

Anti-Terrorism, Crime and Security Act 2001.

The Maguire Case

Introduction

Dicey, the constitutional lawyer, wrote:[1]
"Men legislate…not in accordance with their opinion as to what is a good law, but in accordance with their interest, and this…is emphatically true of classes as contrasted with individuals, and therefore of a country like England, where classes exert a far more potent control over the making of laws than can any single person…So true is this, that from the inspection of the laws of a country it is often possible to conjecture…what is the class which hold, or has held, predominant power at a given time".

The troubles in Northern Ireland erupted in 1969 when Loyalists bombed power stations and civil rights marches and burned Catholic houses and looted shops[2]. By 1971 the Provisional Irish Republican Army viewed the British Army as a force of occupation. In 1972, the IRA brought the war in Ireland onto the streets of Britain.

The Maguire case[3] can be seen as "political"(Darby, Dodge & Hepburn,1990).
The charges brought against the Maguires, possession of explosive substances under suspicious circumstances[4] were a knee-jerk reaction to appease the pub-

---

1. A.V .Dicey, "Law and Public Opinion in England during the nineteenth century", Macmillan Publishers, 1914, pp 12-13.
2. It is to be noted interestingly that this religious fighting happens despite Chapter XII of the Irish Constitution, of which Article 43 (2.1)states "Freedom of conscience and the free profession and practice of religion are, subject to public order and morality, guaranteed to every citizen." (2.2) "The State guarantees not to endow any religion". (2.3) "The State shall not impose any disabilities or make any discrimination on the ground of religious profession, belief or status".
3. Ann Maguire and six other defendants were sentenced to terms of up to 14 years on evidence that was spurious. When the police arrested the people suspected of the bombing in Guildford, it was alleged that they were told that Ann Maguire had taught them to make bombs. They searched her house and found no explosive material or bomb making equipment.

lic who wanted the murderers caught immediately. The inquiry that followed revealed it to be a carelessly constructed case of rebuttable evidence.[5] They could have been charged under the conspiracy law instead. As it was, the Court of Appeal in 1991 found that it could not be proved that Maguire did indeed possess any explosive substances and that the forensic result that concluded at trial that there was explosive substance on Ann Maguire's glove or under her fingernails was an incorrect extrapolation of the forensic test results. The substance on the glove could have been as a result of contamination of the gloves by another person in the forensic laboratory or elsewhere. In fact the police never did find any guns or explosive substances at the Maguires' home. It was found that the confessions were obtained after severe beatings of the defendants by the police.

The writer intends to examine the case as a miscarriage of justice case and follow and examine the legislation and its developments pointing out any reactionary and hastily drafted consequential legislation and its subsequent effect.

Background

Statistics state that, since 1969, eighty-nine people were killed by Irish terrorists in England[6]. Though the IRA's murder rate in England is small compared to that in Northern Ireland, [7]it is likely to remain the main terrorist killer in Great Britain[8].

---

4. Explosive Substances Act 1883,s.4, states:
    "Any person who makes or knowingly has in his possession or under his control any explosive substance, under such circumstances as to give rise to a reasonable suspicion that he is not making it or does not have it in his possession or under his control for a lawful object, shall, unless he can show that he made it or had it in his possession or under his control for a lawful object, be guilty of [an offence].

5. Sir John May, who led the inquiry into the Gulidford bombings, produced his report on the "Maguire Seven" and called it the worst miscarriage of justice he had ever seen.

6. Paper in "British Perspective",1993: Paper by Richard Clutterbuck 'Terrorism in Britain'

7. "Political Violence" edited by Darcy, Dodge & Hepburn,1990, Fatal Incidents 1969-1981 in Derry,Belfast,Armagh,Strabane,Portadown,Dungannon,Lurgan,Newry,Limavady,Carrickfergus, Omagh, Enniskillen, Comber & Ballymoney total 1235.

8. "Terrorism in Britain" paper by Peter Clutterbuck(1993).

In 1974 there were IRA bomb explosions in two public houses. Six persons were convicted on charges of possession of explosives. Twenty one persons had died as a result of bombs in Birmingham. On 4th March 1976 at the Central Criminal Court, Anne Rita Maguire,[9] Patrick Joseph Maguire, Patrick Joseph Conlon, William John Smyth, Vincent John Patrick Maguire, Patrick Joseph Paul Maguire and Patrick Joseph O'Neill were each convicted of a separate count charging an offence contrary to section 4(1) of the Explosive Substances Act 1883. It is to be noted that Patrick Maguire, Ann Maguire's son, was then only thirteen years old and received a four year prison sentence in a Category A high-security cell, as was his mother, father and seventeen-year old brother.

Four persons were charged and convicted of murder in respect of the Guildford bombs.. With regard to the Guildford four case the 1984 inquiry caused a vast pile of documents which were not disclosed at trial. Among these were a set of typewritten records of the Surrey detectives' interviews with Patrick Armstrong one of the defendants convicted of murder. This typewritten record was covered in corrections, additions and rearrangements of material, yet, when the police gave evidence at the Guildford Four trial in 1975, they had presented a set of hand-written notes, which they said, were a verbatim, contemporaneous record made during interview. It was revealed that the manuscript notes were identical to the draft typewritten version. The typescript had preceded the manuscript[10].

Evidence relating to handwriting for the purpose of establishing the identity of the writer, or excluding particular persons from writing it, may be given by experts Yet the expertise of the expert need not have been attained in any particular prescribed manner, a principle explained in the case R v Silverlock [11]

---

9.   In her book, "Miscarriage of Justice, An Irish Family's Story of Wrongful Conviction as IRA Terrorists", Cardinal Basil Hume's foreword included these words:
     'Anne Maguire was caught up in a terrible situation not of her making, accused unjustly of a crime she never committed'.
10. "In the name of the law", David Rose, 1996, Vintage Press.
11. R v Silverlock [1894] 2QB 766

The police officers had seriously misled the court and had colluded with each other to do so. There were undisclosed papers which cast great doubt on the confession taken from Hill. The case had depended on the confessions and upon the integrity of the police officers. The case of the former six was based on scientific evidence that nitro-glycerine had been found on their hands and gloves.

In 1977 the Guildford four convicted of murder had appealed and lost. But there was new evidence submitted in their appeal. It triggered a campaign to have an appeal heard on the case of the Maguire six convicted of handling explosives, after which the Home Secretary Douglas Hurd asked the Avon and Somerset police to re-examine all the evidence of 1977. In 1989 the Court of Appeal quashed the murder convictions of the Guildford four. As a result of these quashed convictions, a judicial inquiry was set up into the case and also into this case of the Maguire six convicted on charges of possession of explosives[12]

Evidence was given during the inquiry to 1989 of the unsafeness of these convictions. The Home Secretary then referred the case of the five appellants (one had died in prison) to the Court of Appeal under Section 17 (1)(a) of the *Criminal Appeal Act 1968*. It is to be noted from the case report that these six had previously, in 1980, sued the police officers for civil damages for beating and threatening them and had lost the case.

At the Appeal, new scientific evidence and more tests carried out since the trial, was compared with the trial evidence.

There were several issues. Was there full disclosure of the scientific evidence at the trial?[13] Is the information provided by expert witnesses sufficient for legal purposes?[14] Were the tests used by the prosecution scientists sufficiently reliable?[15] Were the tests carried out by competent personnel?

---

12. Explosive Substances Act 1883 s3
    Acts done with the specific intent to cause an explosion.
13. Administration of Justice (Miscellaneous Provisions) Act 1933 s2(2)(b).
    The accused is allowed to inspect any prosecution material at a reasonable time and a reasonable place.

The Court of Appeal made a reassessment of the scientific evidence. Much of the questioning of the experts about their evidence at trial was directed at the reliability of the tests used and the interpretation of those tests given by the scientists to the jury at the trial. This undermined the credibility of the Crown expert witnesses showing that they had been selective about the material produced. What they should have produced was the notes and results of tests carried out on actual samples and notes of any experimental tests or trials irrespective of whether the prosecution intended to rely on them or not. It is to be noted that ESDA tests were used to question the validity of the West Midlands Serious Crime Squad and in this year the squad was disabled and the Police Complaints Authority was launched. It was an ESDA test on an interview with the defendant Richard McIlkenny which destroyed the prosecution evidence, and this interview was the only interview in the entire case and it was said to have been written down contemporaneously. That this interview was written down contemporaneously was stated in the original 1975 trial.

The Maguires had been found guilty almost wholly on the basis of forensic evidence.
The principal evidence at trial in this case was the forensic evidence that showed that some of the defendants had been in direct contact with nitroglycerine. The fresh scientific evidence showed that the hands could have been contaminated not by direct contact with explosives but by hands which had been in contact with it. The earlier evidence at trial did not allow the court to conclude who the person or persons were who so contaminated the towel or gloves.

At the trial Mr. Elliot, a Home Office Scientific Officer gave evidence that extensive tests on the Maguires' house had produced no evidence of bulk explosives or detonators. However, tests on the defendants' hands[16], under

---

14. Criminal Justice Act 1948 s41(1)
      Permits statements and drawings exhibited in criminal proceedings to be accepted as evidence.
15. Criminal Justice Act 1967 S(9)
      Admissibility of written statements in proceedings.

their fingernails and on one of the defendants' gloves, had proved positive for nitroglycerine for each of the defendants. [17]

This evidence was supported by two other Home Office scientific officers. Mr.Elliot claimed that a TLC[18] test was unique for nitroglycerine.
It was held on Appeal that there was possibility of the Appellant's hands or gloves having been innocently contaminated with nitroglycerine[19] and therefore the convictions of all the appellants were unsafe and unsatisfactory.[20] This is a case which illustrates that forensic scientists,[21] the police and the prosecution did not only disregard evidence which contradicts their case theory but also kept this from the defence and in turn, the jury.

FORENSIC EVIDENCE

Forensic science is regarded as the employment of particular scientific techniques in the investigation and prosecution of criminal offences. It is scientists acting for the police who almost invariably conduct the initial investigations of which the collection of samples is a crucial part., these samples having been taken at the scene of crime and subsequently in the laboratory. The courts have exercised very little control over this aspect of a prosecution and defence scientists are often unable to test these initial findings.

16. The original swabs that were taken had been lost or destroyed at the government laboratory by the 17 year old technician who had done the analysis.
17. Halsbury's Laws of England, Criminal Law, Evidence and Procedure Volume.
18. Thin Layer Chromatography
19. "English Criminal Appeals" by Rosemary Pattenden, p372:
    'The CACD quashed the convictions of the Maguire family for handling explosives contrary to s4(1) of the Explosive Substances Act 1883 on the sole ground that innocent contamination could not be ruled out'.
20. "English Criminal Appeals" by Rosemary Conley, p 146
    'The meaning of "unsafe" or "satisfactory" has not been closely scrutinised."
21. ibid, p 377, Rosemary Patterden makes an interesting statement of fact that the scientists who carried out or supervised most of the disputed scientific tests were dead by the time the Maguire case came to CACD,ie.15 years after trial.

On March 1st 2001 a Centre for Forensic Statistics and Legal Reasoning was opened as a multi-disciplinary Centre, drawing on the skills in statistics,law and artificial intelligence from the University of Edinburgh and Glasgow Caledonian University working in collaboration with the Lothian Borders Police Forensic Science Laboratory investigate issues such as incorrect use of evidence, unnecessary forensic tests and identifying and addressing possibilities for miscarriage of justice related to the presentation and interpretation of evidence. This is a much needed centre and will be observed closely by all interested in the due process of law, although late in the day.

LEGAL RESPONSE

The Maguire case is one of two cases of bombing incidents in 1974 in which 26 people died. As a direct response to these bombings, there was the enactment of the anti-terrorism legislation, the Prevention of Terrorism (Temporary Provisions) Act 1974[22]. It can be said to be an Act which affected all Irish people as the power of the Act force Irish people, especially, to prove their innocence. "According to a former chairman of the Federation of Irish Societies in Britain, the Act has 'terrified the ordinary Irish people in this country'".[23] Section 1(2) and Schedule 1 proscribe the Irish Republican Army. Section 1(3) empowers the Home Secretary by order to proscribe other organisations. Scope for judicial review of any order has been cut down. The model for Section 1(5) is the Northern Ireland (Emergency Provisions) Act 1973. Section 1(5) makes it an offence punishable on indictment by a maximum term of imprisonment of five years, or a fine of £400 or both, to belong to a proscribed organisation. Section 2 of the Prevention of Terrorism(Temporary Provisions)Act 1974 does what Section 1 of the Public Order Act 1936 failed to do. It provides a comprehensive definition of wearing a uniform. It enacts that (for this Act only):

---

22. PREVENTION OF TERRORISM (Temporary Provisions)ACT 1974 section 12 provides for a person whom a constable has arrested on reasonable grounds of suspecting him to be guilty of an offence under section 1,9 or 10 of the Act, or to be or to have been involved in terrorism connected with the affairs of Northern Ireland, to be detained in right of arrest for up to 48 hours and thereafter where the Secretary of State extends the detention period, for up to a further five days.
23. "Political Trials in Britain", by Peter Hain, 1982 Allen Lane Publishers. Page 229.

"Any person who in a public place—

a.   wears any item of dress ; or

b.   wears, carries or displays any article;

in such a way or in such circumstances as to arouse reasonable apprehension that he is a member or supporter of a proscribed organisation, shall be liable on summary conviction to imprisonment, for a term not exceeding three months or to a fine not exceeding £200 or both." Part II of the Prevention of Terrorism (Temporary Provisions) Act 1974 introduced exclusion orders based on the repealed
Prevention of Violence(Temporary Provisions) Act 1939. An exclusion order always prohibits a person from being in or entering the UK. UK citizens are the only persons exempt (section 3(4)). There is no power of appeal to the courts because exclusion orders are concerned with national security rather than with judicial issues. The Act set up security control over travellers entering or leaving the UK and is modelled on immigration control.

The Prevention of Terrorism Act has been superseded by the new Terrorism Act 2000 which came into force on 19th February 2001. This new Act provides for permanent UK-wide anti-terrorist legislation, a new definition of terrorism, new powers to seize suspected terrorist cash at borders, new judicial arrangements for extensions of detention enabling the United Kingdom to lift its derogations under the European Convention on Human Rights and specific offences relating to training for terrorist activities. This Act enables the police not only to arrest and detain on suspicion of terrorist activities but also to prevent from disclosing such police acts. Section 39 (1 to 4) states :
"Subsection (2) applies where a person knows or has reasonable cause to suspect that a constable is conducting or proposes to conduct a terrorist investigation. the person commits an offence if he—

a.   discloses to another anything which is likely to prejudice the investigation, or

b.   interferes with material which is likely to be relevant to the investigation.

Subsection (4) applies where a person knows or has reasonable cause to suspect that a disclosure has been or will be made under any of sections 19 to 21.

Section (4) states that the person commits an offence if he

a.   discloses to another anything which is likely to prejudice an investigation resulting from the disclosure under that section, or

b.   interferes with material which is likely to be relevant to an investigation resulting from the disclosure under that section."

There are three new UK-Wide Codes of Practice governing the day-to-day operation of the Terrorism Act 2000. These are the Code of Practice for the Audio Recording of Interviews, the Code of Practice for Examining Officers at ports and the Code of Practice for Authorised Officers in respect of the seizure of terrorist cash at ports. Of these, only two Codes of Practice have been brought into force in Northern Ireland: these govern the exercise by police officers of powers conferred under the Act and the sound and vision recording of police interviews.

The Government put out a Consultation Paper about Disclosure Requirements. in 1997. In its response to the Government's Consultation Paper[24] about Disclosure Requirements, the Law Society quotes from the Report of the Royal Commission on Criminal Justice (1993) that "the defence can require the police and prosecution to comb through large masses of material in the hope of causing delay". The Law Society states that there is no evidence to support the allegation that this is the motive behind defence requests for dis-

---

24.   http://www.lawsociety.org.uk/dcs
       'Disclosure : Law Society Responses.
       Responses of the Law Society of England and Wales to the Government Consultation Paper.
       1) Answering the Government's Complaints about the Current Disclosure Requirements.
       2) Why the Government's Aims will risk further miscarriages of Justice.
       3) Reaching a just verdict.
       4) The Police are expected to disclose their own faults.
       5) Misuse of evidence.
       6) "Ambush" Defences.
       7) Simplifying the Trial.
       8) The proposed procedure.
       9) Names and Addresses of Defence Witnesses.
       10)Conclusion.

closure and the judges frequently find it necessary to order disclosure of evidence that is not disclosed voluntarily by the prosecution. It goes on to say that even prosecution forensic evidence is partial and requires a close scrutiny which is possible with full disclosure, although even when full disclosure is found not to have occurred a conviction can still be held, as in the case of Angela Ramden v The State (1999), Privy Council case[25].

There is the Official Secrets Act 1989 (c.6) which replaced section 2 of the Official Secrets Act 1911 by making provisions that protect limited classes of official information. It provides powerful sanctions against leaks of official information which can harm national security. It applies to unauthorised disclosures by civil servants[26] or other who acquire information through official duties such as police, members of armed forces and ministers of the government. Journalists who obtain protected information which has been disclosed without authority commit a criminal offence. Journalists who help a present or retired member of the security or intelligence services to reveal information could be charged as accessories to the officer's offence. It can be argued that the Official Secrets Act also affect the judicial process. Plea bargaining, deals between defence and prosecution, the choice of a judge are not facts that are open to scrutiny before they occur. The Official Secrets Act has a clear politi-

---

25. http://www.privy-council.org.uk
"Privy Council Office Judicial Committee"
Angela Ramdeen v The State from
The Court of Appeal of Trinidad and Tobago.
This is an appeal by special leave from a judgement of the Court of Appeal of Trinidad and Tobago delivered on 15th October 1997 dismissing the appellant's appeal against conviction on two counts of murder. In this case Mr. Justice Henry stated that they were not persuaded that any miscarriage of justice has been demonstrated; that the appellant had a fair trial ; that further evidence does not contain that degree of cogency which gives concern as to the safety of the verdict and that it cannot be said that the evidence is fresh, in the sense of being unavailable at trial.

26. Official Secrets Act 1989. 4(1):
"A person who is or has been a Crown servant or government contractor is guilty of an offence if without authority he discloses any information, document or other article to which this section applies and which is or has been in his possession by virtue of his position as such."

cal purpose. Terrorist outrages by the IRA are to be vigorously and absolutely condemned but also are the abuses of power by the security authorities.

As a direct result of the Maguire Appeal Case there was enacted the Criminal Appeal Act 1995 which removes the power of the Home Secretary[27] to investigate and refer to the Court of Appeal under Section 17 of the Criminal Appeal Act 1968. The Criminal Appeal Act 1995 received the Royal Assent on 19th July 1995. Section 1 brings appeals against conviction on a question of law alone into line with other appeals against conviction or sentence by requiring leave to appeal except where the trial judge has certified that the case is fit for appeal.. Section 2 abolishes the proviso[28] and substitutes for the 3 grounds for allowing an appeal, a single ground that the Court of Appeal thinks that the conviction is unsafe. Section 55 gives the Court the power to carry out or direct the Criminal Cases Review Commission to carry out investigations and to report to the Court. Section 13 of the Criminal Appeal Act 1995 prohibits the Commission from referring a case to the Court of Appeal unless it considers that there is a real possibility that the Court of Appeal will quash the conviction.

Section 13 transfers this task to the Criminal Cases Review Commission. Appendix 1 shows the activity of this Commission with total applications of 4605 cases 3808 cases completed to January 2002. That there have been 4605 applications presented to the Criminal Cases Review Commission between 1997 and 2002 is a damning indictment on the inefficiency of the criminal justice system.

The Home Secretary can still refer a case for investigation with a view to offering a pardon[29]. The original power to direct others to investigate can be found in section 9(d) of the Criminal Appeal Act 1907[30].

Another enactment is the Criminal Justice and Public Order Act 1994[31]

---

27. Section 3 Criminal Appeal Act 1995
28. Section 2(1) Criminal Appeal Act 1968 lays down 3 conditions on which an appeal must be allowed.
29. Section 3 Criminal Appeal Act 1995
30. Section 3 Criminal Appeal Act 1995

Paragraph 62 of schedule 10 to the CJPOA 1994 contains detailed provisions for the application of modified forms of the amended provisions of PACE, ss 62 and 63. to persons arrested or detained under the terrorism provisions. Also PACE s 64, providing for the destruction of fingerprints and samples does not apply to persons detained under these provisions. Police Code of Practice C provides that, if it is proposed to question a juvenile, mentally disordered or mentally handicapped person the police must inform an appropriate adult (eg social worker) and ask him to come to the police station to see the person. The appropriate adult is allowed to consult privately with the person and to be present during any interview and these rights are additional to the normal right to legal advice. One of the defendants, Richardson was a mentally handicapped person. She was given no appropriate adult to help her and was instead made to take an opiate drug, an injection of pethedine, before she made a confession. Research by Gudjonsson et al, 1993 Research Study No.12 "Persons at risk during interviews in Police Custody: The identification of vulnerabilities", show that the police fail to recognise some suspects as mentally disordered, classifying as "vulnerable" only about a quarter of those who actually are. The Royal Commission in its Criminal Justice Report paragraph 3.86, recommends that section 77 of the 1984 Police and Criminal Evidence Act, on the inadmissibility of confessions made in the absence of an independent person, should be extended from the mentally handicapped to cover all mentally disordered suspects. It is to be noted that, with regard to serious mistreatment of suspects, the European Court of Justice found in Ireland v UK[32], that there was a violation of Article 3 of the European Convention on Human Rights, when the evidence disclosed severe beatings of four detainees by Northern Ireland security forces.[33] In the Ireland v UK case, it was disclosed that there were five common practices in use in Northern Ireland that were inhuman. They were wall-standing for long periods, hooding, subjection to noise, sleep deprivation and deprivation of food and drink.[34]. Under the Police and Criminal Evidence Act 1984, section 78, confessions after such interview-

31. The Criminal Cases Review Commission is made up of eleven members, one third being lawyers and the rest lay members.
32. Ireland v UK A25 (1978)
33. "Criminal Justice and the Human Rights Act 1998" by D. Cheney, L, Dickson, J. Fitzpatrick and S. Uglow, 1999,Jordans Publishers.
34. ibid

ing techniques would be inadmissible. But there are inconsistencies in the law in that although PACE would now apply for matters of confession, PACE, sections 40 to 43, do not apply in terrorism cases in which more time is needed for interrogation. PACE ss40-42 comply with Article 5(3) of the European Convention of Human Rights, but since the case of Brogan v UK [35], the government has issued a notice of derogation from Article 5(3) in respect of terrorism cases.

On Saturday 1st, September 2001 the Criminal Justice and Police Act 2001 became effective. Part 4 of the Act concerns police training.. It establishes a Central Police Training and Development Authority and stipulates the function of that Authority as being, to provide police training and facilities for the provision of police training, to promote the value of the provision of this training, to give advice in this regard and to advice and act as a consultancy with regard to best police practice and handling of incidents requiring police involvement. Driving up standards is at the heart of this police reform. It is to be seen whether this new regime of police training will eliminate all the deficiencies in police behaviour as set out in The Royal Commission's Research Reports of 1993 and stem the atrocious wrong-doings that occurred in the Maguire pre-trial period.

The Anti-Terrorism, Crime and Security Act 2001 is a new Act which will take the form of a Code of practice relating to communications data held by data providers. This will hopefully aid national security. It can be argued that it will provide all sorts of hear-say and unsubstantiated data and may be seen as an attempt to snoop on the nation's emails. This may lead to more wrongful arrests.

There is the enactment is the Criminal Procedure and Investigations Act 1996. Part 1 of this Act creates a new scheme for compulsory pre-trial disclosure. The prosecution has a duty to disclose under the firm supervision of the courts[36]. Part II of the Act regulates the retention and disclosure of material collected by the police in the course of criminal investigations. If there is

---

35. Brogan v UK A/145-B, 11 EHRR 117 (1988)
36. Page 219 "Understanding Miscarriages of Justice" Richard Nobles & David Schieff (2000),Oxford University Press.

doubt as to the relevance of material, the prosecution may place the material before the court for a decision on disclosure[37]

This disclosure regime was presented to Parliament as a scheme designed to secure efficiency and sound judicial administration of the criminal trial process by early identification of issues and as a way of eliminating unjustifiable defence tactics resulting in unmerited acquittals (Owen,2001).[38]

Furthermore, in applying the interpretative obligation in section 3 of the Human Rights Act 1998 to the wording of section 3 of the CPIA 1996, it is likely that the courts will conclude that the primary disclosure obligation on the prosecution authorities involves a return to the principles in R v Keane[39]. The CIPA 1996 regime with its carrot and stick approach to disclosure, clearly indicated an intention to sanction the with-holding of relevant material at the primary disclosure stage.[40]

Another disclosure rule since the Maguire case is the Magistrates' Courts (Advance Notice of Expert Evidence) Rules 1997 SI 1997/705, made under the Magistrates' Courts Act 1984 section 144. Also, the Criminal Procedure and Investigations Act 1996 section 20 (3) (4) states that where a magistrates' court proceeds to summary trial in respect of an alleged offence and the person charged with the offence pleads not guilty in respect of it, if any party to the proceedings proposes to submit expert evidence in the proceedings, he must furnish the other party or parties with a statement in writing of any finding or opinion which he proposes to submit.

---

37. Criminal Justice and Public Order Act 1994
    This Act places a duty on the accused to disclose aspects of his defence to the Police and to penalize the silent. The test for what must be disclosed is materiality, defined by Lord Taylor in Keane [1994]1WLR 746, section 32.
    Judge retains a discretion to use caution in regard to uncorroborated testimony.
38. "Criminal Justice, Police Powers and Human Rights",2001,K.Starmer,etc.,Blackstone Press, p132.
39. R v Keane (1994)1WLR 746.
40. ibid, pg 40

THE HUMAN RIGHTS ACT 1998 ultimately provides a remedy for individuals. It empowers a court to grant such relief or remedy or to make such order within its powers as it considers just and appropriate, including the award of damages. If damages are awarded, it must take into account the principles applied by the European Court in awarding them. Section 10 and Schedule 2 of the Human Rights Act 1998 confers crucial and very considerable power on a minister of the government to amend primary and subordinate legislation by order. That power can be triggered in two ways: first, when a court makes a declaration of incompatibility under section 4 between domestic legislation and a Convention rights, and secondly, when the European Court makes a finding (after this section comes into force) which leads a government minister to believe that a provision of domestic legislation is incompatible with UK obligations under the Convention.

Police and Criminal Evidence Act

The subject of evidence is emotive. There are those who follow the legal philosopher Bentham who represents one extreme, i.e. "the elevation of the truth in the adjudication above nearly all other competing claims of value or policy; the principle that inferior or otherwise defective evidence is better than no evidence; the evaluation of weight and credibility to be left to the discretion of the ultimate decision-maker, who is expected to proceed rationally and efficiently largely unconfined by formal rules…"
And there are those who support Wigmore's "science of proof".

The rules of evidence which apply in a criminal trial are substantially the same as those which apply in a civil action but the distinctions are a higher standard of proof and the need to prevent the introduction of unfair or prejudicial evidence before a jury or magistrates. With regard to evidence, contemporary documents are of the greatest probative value. If evidence relative to the issues can be reduced to that in written form, so much the better. The more the evidence is in written form, the shorter and more predictable the trial will be as the issues as to facts are narrowed. There are ESDA tests used to question the validity of written evidence. Even when evidence such as original interview notes are shredded, and this is illegal, as police pocketbooks are not allowed by law to be shredded until after six years, and other documentary evidence in a police inquiry are governed by the 1958 and 1967 Public Records Acts, missing documents are commonly indicated by references in surviving documents.

The deliberate decision to destroy relevant documents when proceedings are imminent or after their commencement involves the criminal offence of obstructing or perverting the course of justice. R v Selvage[41] and R v Rowell.[42]

The general rules of evidence[43] state that the prosecution is required to disclose to the accused unused material which might undermine the prosecution case, including material they should not have in their possession, such as compiled records kept on computers and between forces[44] and the accused is required to disclose the general nature of his defence, following which, the prosecution is required to make further disclosure of such additional unused material as might assist that defence[45].

Traditionally, the investigation of serious crime involves the police in the examination of the crime scene and the analysis of forensic evidence, the use of house-to-house enquiries, the questioning of witnesses and suspects, stopping and searching persons and vehicles, mounting road blocks and arresting and detaining and interviewing suspects. The basic powers of the police to undertake such actions are now mainly contained within the Police and Criminal Evidence Act 1984 and its amendments which has codified the law on police powers. Nothing in the PACE 1984 prejudices any power of a court to exclude evidence. The court retains a general discretion to exclude prosecution evidence. As a general rule the evidence which must be adduced is restricted to evidence of those matters tending directly or indirectly to prove or disprove the facts in issue. In a criminal trial the prosecution must prove that the offence alleged has been committed by some person and that that person was

---

41. R v Selvage (!982) QB 372
42. R v Rowell (1978) 1 WLR 132
43. Criminal Procedure and Investigations Act 1996 (ss 1-21), paragraph 1055A
44. Police Review May 1972
    "Since 1966, the Service has collaborators in most police divisions and they have amassed information which in both quantity and quality would surprise most people on their books....There is a serious chance that once a person is in the system, he may remain there......"
45. http://disraeli.butterworths.co.uk/wbs/NETbos.
    Halsbury's Laws of England, Criminal Law, Evidence and Procedure, 13. Evidence.

the accused. In proving the alleged offence it may be relevant to go beyond proof of the unlawful act itself to show that other conduct or surrounding circumstances which are connected with the offence and to make them part of the same transaction. So all the details of the alleged transaction may become relevant so as to be admissible as part of the prosecution's case.

The Maguire case hinged on forensic evidence. There are a number of types of scientific evidence which are routinely admitted in criminal proceedings. Examples are the analysis of fibres and hairs, blood/alcohol levels, drugs and glass, the grouping of blood stains and the investigation of arson. The categories of admissible scientific evidence are not closed. A discipline, such as the testing for nitro-glycerine in the Maguire case, need not be simply accepted or rejected for evidential purposes. It may have a limited use in the court process because of its limitations. A scientific technique may be treated as admissible but subject to specific warnings to lay triers of fact as to the need for clearly understood and forensically unambiguous results.(Taylor v O'Connor[1971] Ac 115.) PACE 1984 is a statutory code of police powers of arrest, search and questioning, supported by Codes of Practice issued by the Home Office. The Maguire case police investigation confirmed to practically none of the procedures in the present Police and Criminal Evidence Act. and the defendants also had almost all of their human rights violated

Police powers can interfere with the liberty of the subject and must comply with Article 5 of the European Convention on Human Rights. Basic traditional practices such as the right to ask for a solicitor when arrested. One of the reasons for allowing suspects the right to consult with a solicitor at a police station is to ensure that the conduct of the police towards the suspect is scrupulously fair. The Maguires were not given this right as they would have, had the investigation occurred in 1984 and not 1974.

A police investigation is designed to produce evidence in subsequent proceedings and the most significant reason to attack the conduct of that investigation is to seek to exclude that evidence in the course of any subsequent trial. There are human rights which arise under Article 5 or 8 relating to pre-trial process. Pre-trial issues impact on the trial.

CONCLUSION

The authority of the legal system is uncontested when it comes to the question of the validity of rules. The validity of facts should be primary in arriving at legal decisions, not secondary. There are no clearly circumscribed conditions for reopening cases of miscarriages of justice. This is as well, because it gives the flexibility needed to achieve real fairness, individual rights and due process of law. It is evident that further reforms are necessary and perhaps an appeal process that is capable of correcting unjust verdicts quickly and effectively when they do occur.

But ultimately, it is faulty police performance which undermines the criminal justice system. The police need closer monitoring and re-investigation procedures.

There are many issues in investigation of crime. Firstly, the Police and Criminal Evidence Act 1984, section 24, provides that a police officer may arrest any person whom he has reasonable grounds to suspect of having committed an offence. Arrest is not the only way of beginning an investigation into the involvement of a suspect, but it is the most coercive. In practice, detention following arrest seems to be authorised as a matter of routine and there is not usually fresh application of the "necessity principle" by the police custody officer. The other practice is to make an arrest but to rely on the "voluntary" attendance of the suspect at a police station. Failure to read the defendant's rights is also prevalent. Police Code of Practice C provides that, if it is proposed to question a mentally handicapped person, the police must inform an appropriate adult. Richardson, Hill and Conlon in the Birmingham Six case had supported alibis and there was medical evidence of Richardson's suggestibility. It emerged that Richardson was given an injection by the police of the opiate drug pethidene before she made her confession. There was a vast pile of documents extant from the 1974 enquiry. This type of miscarriage of justice by inappropriate activities is targeted for correction by the new Criminal Justice and Police Act 2001, in force since 1st September 2001,which stipulates Police Training Regulations. Section 87 of the Act states :
"(1) There shall be a body corporate to be known as the Central Police Training and Development Authority.
(2) Schedule 3 (which makes provision about the Authority) shall have effect."

This new Authority aims to be a centre of excellence on police training and operational policy. A Standards Unit aims to have a significant role in identifying areas for improvement in training and a new Police Leadership development Board aims to ensure that the necessary leadership skills are reflected in training and development for all ranks in the police as well as for civilian support staff in leadership roles. Chief police officers will be appraised for the first time. This massive police reform aims to drive up standards. It is to be seen whether this Act brings about fundamental change in many aspects of policing and a more effective attack on crime in the future with less miscarriages of justice and more of the evidentially supported actual perpetrators of serious crimes convicted. But it remains to be seen whether legislation will really change entrenched police habits and attitudes.

TABLE OF CASES

Brogan v UK A/145-B, 11EHRR 117 (1988)
Ireland v UK A25 (1978)
R v Maguire and others (1991) CA
Ramdeen v State of Trinidad & Tobago,(1999) Privy Council.
R v Keane (1994)WLR 746
R v Selvage (1982) QB 372
R v Silverlock [1894] 2Qb 766
R v Rowell (1978) 1WLR 132

TABLE OF STATUTES

1. Administration of Justice (Miscellaneous Provisions) Act 1933.

2. Administration of Justice Act 1996.

3. Criminal Appeal Act 1995.

4. Criminal Evidence Act 1898.

5. Criminal Evidence Act 1968.

6. Criminal Justice Act 1987.

7. Criminal Justice Act 1988.

8. Criminal Justice Act 1991.

9. Criminal Justice and Police Act 2001.

10. Criminal Justice and Public Order Act 1994.

11. Criminal Law Act 1967.

12. Criminal Law Act 1977.

13. Criminal Procedure Act 1865.

14. Criminal Procedure and Investigations Act 1996.

15. The European Convention on Human Rights

16. Interception of Communications Act 1985

17. Human Rights Act 1998..

18. Magistrates Courts Act 1980.

19. Magistrates Courts (Advance Notice of Expert Evidence) Rules 1997

20. Northern Ireland (Emergency Provisions) Act 1973.

21. Official Secrets Act 1989

22. Police and Criminal Evidence Act 1984.

23. Prevention of Violence (Temporary Provisions) Act 1939.

24. Public Order Act 1936.

25. Terrorism Act 2000.

26. Anti-Terrorism, Crime and Security Act 2001.

BIBLIOGRAPHY

1. R v Maguire & Others (1992)

2. Halsbury's Laws of England, Criminal Law, Evidence and Procedure. http://www.lawsociety.org.uk

3. "Disclosure :Law Society Responses".

4. "Civil Liberties & Human Rights in England & Wales",D. Feldman (1993), Clarendon Press, Oxford.

5. "Criminal Law-Essays in Honour of J.C.Smith", editor Peter Smith(1987), Butterworths.

6. The Criminal Process—an evaluative study", Andrew Ashworth (1995),Oxford University Press.

7. "Justice and Efficiency? The Royal Commission on Criminal Justice", edited by Stewart Field and Philip A. Thomas (1994),Blackwell Publishers.

8. "Suspicion & Silence. The Right to Silence in Criminal Investigations", edited by David Morgan & Geoffery Stephenson (1994), Blackstone Press.

9. "The Royal Commission on Criminal Justice—The conduct of Police Investigations :Records of Interview, the Defence Lawyer's Role and Standards of Supervision. Research Study No.2,3 and 4., (1993) HMSO.

10. "The Royal Commission on Criminal Justice. The Questioning and Interviewing of Suspects Outside the Police Station. Research Study No.22.(1993) HMSO.

11. "Cases and Statutes on Criminal Procedure", A.K. Mughal,(1973), Butterworths.

12. "Critical Legal Studies", edited by Peter Fitzpatrick & Alan Hunt,(1990), Blackwell Press.

13. "Criminal Justice and the Human Rights Act 1998".,by Deborah Cheyney, Lisa Dickson, John Fitzpatrick & Steve Uglow, (1999), Jordans Press.

14. http://www.privy-council.org.uk
    "Privy Council Office Judicial Committee".

15. http://www.ccre.gov.up/management
    "Criminal Cases Review Commission—Management Statement".

16. http://www.butterworthsireland.com/newsdirect
    "Court declares miscarriage of justice in Tallaght Two case".

17. http://www.leeds.ac.uk/law
    "Victims of miscarriages of justice. Section 133 Criminal Justice Act 1988".

18. http://www.freenetpages.co.uk
    "Lord Lane—the Lord Chief Justice 1980–1993
    R v Anthony Mycock"

19. "Butterworths Police Law", by Jack English & Richard Card, (1996), Butterworths.

20. "Understanding Miscarriages Of Justice", by Richard Nobles & David Schiff, (2000), Oxford University Press.

21. "Criminal Justice & Public Order Act 1994", by Martin Wasik & Richard Taylor,(1995), Blackstone Publishers.

22. "Criminal Procedure & Investigations Act 1996",by Roger Leng & Richard Taylor, (1996), Blackstone Publishers.

23. "Expert Evidence" by Tristram Hodgkinson,1990, Sweet & Maxwell Publishers.

24. "Theories of Evidence : Bentham & Wigmore" by William Twining,1985, Weidenfeld & Nicolson Publishers.

25. "The psychology of Criminal Justice" by Jeoffrey Stephenson,1992,Blackwell Publishers.

26. http://www.legislation.hmso.gov.uk/acts
    The Terrorism Act 2000.

27. http://www.legislation.hmso.gov.uk/acts
    Criminal Justice and Police Act 2001.

28. http://www.aiai.ed.ac.uk
    Centre for Forensic Statistics and Legal Reasoning.

29. http://www.ccrc.gov.uk
    Criminal Cases Review Commission
    Provisional Figures to 31st January 2002.

30. "Blackstone's Criminal Practice 2002", Oxford University Press.

31. "Political Violence. Ireland in a Comparative Perspective", edited by J. Darby, N. Dodge, & A. C. Hepburn, 1990, Appletree Press.

32. "Political Violence and the Law in Ireland", G. Hogan & C. Walker, 1989, Manchester University Press.

33. "Terrorism: British Perspective", edited by P. Wilkinson, 1993, Dartmouth Press.

34. "Conspiracy—Law, Class & Society", by R.Spicer,1981, Lawrence & Wishert Press.

35. "Evidence, cases and materials" edited by M. Ockelton,1991,Butterworths.

36. "English Criminal Appeals 1844–1994", Rosemary Pattenden, 1996, Oxford University Press.

37. "Criminal Justice and the Human Rights Act 1998" by Cheyney, Dickson, Fitzpatrick and Uglow, 1999, Jordans Publishers.

38. http://www.sciences.demon.co.uk
    "Laboratory News, 18th July, 1991" Brian J Ford—misuse of forensic science

39. http://www.innocent.org.uk/books
    "Miscarriages of Justice" by Bob Woffinden

40. http://www.hrw.org/reports, "Northern Ireland:Human Rights Abuses By All Sides" and "Freedom of Expression in the UK".

41. "The Law of Human Rights", by Richard Clayton & Hugh Tomlinson,(2000) Sweet & Maxwell.

ESSAY 6: PRISONERS' RIGHTS IN UNITED KINGDOM PRISONS

PRISONERS' RIGHTS IN UNITED KINGDOM PRISONS

INTRODUCTION

When a person is sent to prison, quite a lot of his civil liberties are curtailed—he cannot leave the prison, has to abide by the regime of the prison authorities without his freedom of choice, is locked up for many hours without exercise or movement, is unable to carry on with his usual profession or trade, loses the choice of association with whomsoever he wishes to and must, if he is allowed, only associate with other prisoners; he cannot enjoy his usual choice of food, leisure amenities, environment, clothes, communication and consumption; he loses his freedom of expression as he must confirm to what is allowed to be said in prison and loses his dignity by having to share primitive toilet facilities with the rest of the prison, to list but a few of the liberties he loses.

This essay will explore the loss of freedom to communicate, freedom to found a family, freedom to be with children and loss of conjugal rights of the prisoner, using caselaw to illustrate that the prisoner does indeed forfeit many important rights, the loss of some of these liberties being quite inhuman and that such losses can be alleged to contravene the UK Human Rights Act 1998 and the European Convention on Human Rights 1950, to which the UK is a party.

Fear of punishment, i.e. fear of the loss of freedoms, is only one way of trying to achieve the result of offenders of laws becoming law-abiding. Punishment by imprisonment can be said to be morally problematic because it involves the infliction of mental pain and physical suffering. But it can be argued that this is for the collective good of society because crime is wrong-doing which deserves censure. The penal system has massive powers that remove much civil liberties from prisoners. Punishment is, however, required by justice, since law-abiding citizens suffer injustice if offenders are allowed to get away with their unfair advantage. On the other hand, people who breach the law are sent to prison, but they usually have a multitude of social and emotional problems which might be cured by addressing their medical conditions, if any, and their

The grounds for the prison restriction on conjugal rights were given by a member State government as that it is justified for the prevention of disorder or crime and that permitting the exercise of conjugal rights in prison, together with the privacy that this would involve, would endanger the security of the prison.[2] This is presumed to be similar grounds for this loss of civil liberty by UK prisoners also.

Inhuman treatment of prisoners: breach of ECHR Convention

Whist it can be argued that the deprivation of liberty is the prison punishment, imprisonment should not be inhuman and should not fail to respect the dignity of the person.

Examples of inhuman treatment are prisoners held in isolation, malnutrition, prisoners deprived of natural light or exercise and denial of family visits and prisoners kept without heat or cleanliness where this threatens their physical and mental health.

The UK is party to the European Convention on Human Rights and Article 3 covers the treatment of prisoners. There is also the United Nations Standard Minimum Rules for the Treatment of Prisoners and the European Prison Rules which were both adopted by the UK.

It can be said with certainty that all UK prisoners forfeit the right and civil liberty of desirable levels of sanitation[3], of maintaining family contact and of freedom to communicate because these are losses incorporated into the Prison Rules. In the 1990 Report of the Committee for the Prevention of Torture and Inhuman or Degrading Treatment, a number of criticisms were made of UK prisons being overcrowded, unsanitary in the slopping out of and defecating in buckets, lack of decency in toilet facilities where there were any, and inadequate exercise and work facilities.

The UK's current legal regime for prisons is governed by the Prison Act 1952 and the Prison Rules 1964. Whilst these can be said to be operational matters of a prison regime, the UK has nevertheless been found in breach of the ECHR Convention many times in cases brought by prisoners.

---

2.   X v Switzerland.
3.   In the case Brady v UK

But the Human Rights Committee has stressed that the obligation to treat persons deprived of their liberty with dignity and humanity is a fundamental and universally acceptable rule, not dependent on the material resources available to the State party.[4]

It can be argued that a prison sentence is in effect the punishment the courts give to offenders of the law and therefore punishment in prison is further punishment to the punishment of depriving someone of their freedom of movement.

Incentives and Earned Privileges Scheme

The UK now has an "Incentives and Earned Privileges Scheme" in force under which prisoners' previous rights, such as family visits, access to private monies, association times[5], wearing of a prisoner's own clothes and community visits now have to be earned based on behaviour in the system; this is an extension of the Prison Rules 1964.[6]. However, there are some basic civil liberties that should never be forfeited nor be incentivised nor earned., such as the freedom of thought, conscience and religion, according to Article 9 of ECHR, and this includes the right to change one's religion or belief in public or private. The right to uphold religious belief, whether in prison or not, is absolute.

The cases that come to court as a result of this incentive scheme are awaited. One relevant past case in this respect is the case of Raymond v Honey.[7] Raymond was engaged in legal proceedings and wrote letters to his solicitors from prison. These letters were read by the Prison Governor and were stopped from being sent. As a result of that incident, Raymond prepared a statement, an unsworn affidavit, a bundle of exhibits and a covering letter in order to apply to the courts to have the Prison Governor committed to prison for contempt. He gave the documents to the prison authorities to be forwarded to the

---

4.   Mukong v Cameroon No.458/1991, UN Doc.CCPR/C/51/D/458/
       1991.
5.   See the case Golder v UK.
6.   Prison Rules 1964—Part 1, section 4—Privileges.
7.   Raymond v Honey, House of Lords [1983]

Crown Office at the Royal Courts of Justice. The Prison Governor also stopped those documents being sent to the Crown Office.

The Courts decided that, at common law, conduct calculated to prejudice a party's access to the courts or to obstruct or interfere with the due course of justice or the lawful process of the courts was a contempt of court; that there was nothing in the Prison Act 1952 that conferred powers to make regulations which would deny or interfere with, the right of a convicted prisoner to have unimpeded access to the courts. The Prison Governor's action was a contempt of court. Lord Wilberforce, in this case, said "A convicted prisoner, in spite of his imprisonment, still retains all his civil rights which have not been taken away expressly, or by necessary implication".

Medical treatment of prisoners

If a prisoner is ill, be it mentally or physically, he should always have the right to be treated immediately and appropriately. In a case before the Court of Justice in Strasbourg, Paul and Audrey Edwards sued the UK Government for failing to protect their mentally ill son Christopher, who was knifed and beaten to death in prison by his cell-mate. They won this case. The Strasbourg Court ruled that the UK authorities failed to protect the life of Christopher Edwards and failed to give his family proper access to an open and rigorous investigation and remedy.

Another case on these grounds is the case of Brooks v Home Office[8] in which a pregnant woman prisoner[9] was deprived of immediate medical treatment and lost one of her baby twins. The prisoner was pregnant and this was a high-risk pregnancy and she was expecting twins. One baby was still-born and

---

8.   Brooks v Home Office TLR 17/2/99.
     This case was an action in negligence by a prisoner against the Home Office for damages for psychiatric injury and loss of her unborn baby while she was in a prison hospital. An ultrasound scan had shown during the twin pregnancy that one twin was 20% smaller than the other and had not grown sufficiently. The doctor in charge failed to seek immediate specialist obstetric advice and allowed five days to pass before the prisoner was given specialist attention.
9.   Home Office Research Study 1997:
     61% of the 1,766 women in prison were pregnant or mothers of children

the prisoner sued the Home Office for medical negligence. She won the case in that it was held that she was entitled to expect the same high care standard as of those free pregnant women. However, she was not awarded damages because it was deemed that a five-day delay in obtaining specialist advice would not have been a breach of duty and that the still-birth was not so caused!

Pregnant women are allowed by law to have their children with them until the children are eighteen months old and there is no discretionary deviation from this, regardless of the impact of the separation at this time upon the mother and the child. It can be argued that the application of this policy is unlawful under the new Human Rights Act, Schedule 1, article 8. The Prison Act 1952 is a very mechanical law and although a woman prisoner is a criminal and must therefore forfeit some civil liberties, this causes the child to forfeit most of the child's civil liberties. There is also a public interest factor here in that this scars the child psychologically for life. A recent case on this matter is R (P) v Secretary of State [10] It was held that the Prison Service was entitled to have a policy that children should cease to reside with their mothers in prison. This sort of challenge may be brought in the future, not as a challenge to the Prison policy on the matter, but on the merit of an individual case that a child's welfare is seriously at risk from the separation from the mother.

Conclusion

We are a long way from the time when prison is replaced by something that will improve society, when the determination of responsibility and the handing down of penalties of imprisonment is replaced by the diagnosis of social illness and the prescription of appropriate medicinal procedures by social scientists. We live in a complex society governed by laws imposed on us for the common good of that society and to ensure that all can enjoy many civil liberties, we must tow the line. It can be argued that our penal system is a just one, and it can be argued that he who does harm must suffer harm by way of losing his liberties. But imprisonment and all its realities as illustrated in the cases discussed, illustrate that imprisonment should have as its primary purpose the prevention of people from becoming criminals. It can be argued that over-crowding[11], the loss of the discussed liberties and many more, do not achieve

---

10. R(P) v Secretary of State [2001] 1WLR 2002-07-04

the result that imprisonment set out to achieve in theory, but instead, creates a cesspit of bitterness, brutality, stress and ignorance which does not bode well for the person who finishes his sentence and re-enters society. The imposition of sanctions does have effect on people's behaviour but imprisonment should always be humane.

11. 71,000 people are in prison in the UK in 2002. Home Office Statistics.

ESSAY 7: PRIVACY AND PRESS FREEDOM IN THE UNITED KINGDOM

Table of Cases

Table of Statutes and Conventions

European Convention on Human Rights 1950

Human Rights Act 1998

Table of Reports, Codes, etc.

Broadcasting Standards Commission Code of Practice

Press Commission's Press Code

Press Complaints Commission Code of Practice

PRIVACY AND PRESS FREEDOM IN THE UNITED KINGDOM

Introduction

The UK has now enacted the Human Rights Act 1998 but the debate on how best to create a satisfactory right to respect for private and family life still continues. This same Act gives the Press freedom of expression, yet there are proposals to regulate the Press further, even though, until recently, it was thought that the Press should regulate itself as regards protection of privacy, rather than using civil or criminal sanctions. Self-discipline was preferred to court regulation in order to preserve Press freedom.
There are also proposals for a statutory tort of "invasion of privacy".

There are proposals to remedy various kinds of intrusion made with the intent to obtain personal material for publication.

The development of the Press Commission and the Broadcasting Commission will be explored to analyse whether this self-regulation is enough, with relevant case law considered.

The merits and de-merits of a proposed tort of invasion of privacy will be discussed and the law as it stand in respect of breach of confidence and the ability of this tort to balance Press freedom with personal information and other privacy issues will be analysed.

The Press Complaints Commission Code of Practice

The Press Council, created in 1953, issued guidelines on privacy and adjudicated on complaints about the Press. It could censure a newspaper and require its adjudication to be published. It was found that this had a number of deficiencies and that its decisions were inconsistent and/or ineffective as it had no power to fine or award an injunction. It was seen as too lenient and its agreement that some disclosures should be in the public interest was uncertain. This finding should however be seen in the light of the good that journalists do, as Lord Simon of Glaisdale of the House of Lords said in his summing up in the *Thalidomide case*[1] : "...People cannot adequately influence the decisions which affect their lives unless they can be adequately informed on the facts and arguments relevant to the decisions. Much of such fact-finding and argumentation necessarily has to be conducted vicariously, the public press being a principal instrument………"

In 1972 the Younger Committee recommended a number of proposals for greater protection from intrusion by the Press but these were not implemented. In 1970 a Committee on Privacy and Related Matters was formed (called Calcutt 1) to improve press self-regulation. In 1991 the Press Complaints Commission was created and agreed a Code of Practice which newspapers accepted. So there still is self-regulation of the Press in the UK. The Code of Practice makes special mention of hospitals and requires that the Press must obtain permission in order to interview patients. It also, like the Press Council, has limited sanctions. After self-regulation under the code had been in place, Sir David Calcutt 's report reviewed its success and found that "….the Press Complaints Commission does not hold the balance fairly between the Press and the individual…it is in essence a body set up by the industry."(Calcutt 2) He proposed the introduction of a statutory tribunal to draw up a Code of Practice for the Press. This was rejected but a Press Commission was set up to monitor a Press Code and this Commission does have powers to fine and award compensation. This Calcutt 2 report also recommended that there should be a tort of breach of privacy.

The Broadcasting Standards Commission

In 1996 this Commission took the role of trying to ensure that broadcasters avoid the unwarranted infringement of privacy in the making and broadcast of radio and television programs. It also issues a Code with which broadcasters are expected to comply. But it has clashed over the privacy issue in the case *Broadcasting Complaints Commission ex parte Granada Television Ltd*[2] The issue was not whether material was or was not in the public domain, but whether by

---

1. Attorney General v Times Newspaper Ltd (1973) 3All ER 54
2. R v Broadcasting Complaints Commision, ex parte Granada Television Ltd TLR 16/12/94
    Granada Television challenged a finding of the BBC that matters already in the public domain could, if re-published, constitute an invasion privacy. In judicial review proceeding, it was found that privacy differed from confidentiality and went well beyond it because it was not confined to secrets.

being published, it caused hurt and anguish. It was found in this case that the British Broadcasting corporation (BBC) had not acted unreasonably in the Wednesbury sense in taking the view that privacy had been invaded.

The merits of a privacy tort that protects against Press intrusion.

If there is to be a privacy tort, it should only relate to personal information which was published without authorisation. In Calcutt 1 such information was defined as those aspects of an individual's life which a reasonable person would assume should remain private. There was a Green Paper which proposed that the tort of privacy could cover any invasion of privacy causing substantial distress. The Green Paper suggested a defence of public interest which would cover the same areas as those related to criminal liability. It suggested that it would be a defence to show that the act in question was done for the purpose of preventing, detecting or exposing the commission of a crime or other seriously anti-social conduct; or for the purpose of preventing the public from being misled by some public statement or action of the individual concerned. This is interesting because these defences are the same as can be found in the self-regulated Press Complaints Commission Code of Conduct.[3]

So if the Code of Conduct works then there is no need for a statute on the subject. This supports the objection made by Lord Chancellor Lord Kilmuir in 1961 to Lord Mancroft's Right of Privacy Bill. Lord Kilmuir said "It is not possible to define in an Act of Parliament the circumstances in which...a defence based on public interest is to be available without either destroying the effectiveness of the right of action or imposing a new and severe restriction on publication generally and the freedom of the press......"

However, there are certain clear invasions of privacy which merit a tort of breach of privacy to be put on the statute books. These are as follows:

---

3.   The Press Code of Practice states:
     Clauses 4,5,7,8 and 9 create exception which may be covered by evoking the public interest. For the purpose of this code that is most easily defined as:
     i) Detecting or exposing crime or a serious misdemeanour.
     ii) Protecting public health or safety.
     iii) Preventing the public being misled by some treatment or action of an individual or organisation

- physical intrusion by reporters both onto the individual's own property or onto other private property where he or she happens to be, as in the case of *Kaye v Robertson (1990)*[4]

- the taking of photographs for publication without the person's consent as in *Campbell v MGN (2002)*[5]

- the use of bugging devices by the press, as in the instance of the former Member of Parliament David Mellor, when the property in which he was regularly having a sexual affair with an actress, was bugged, albeit with her consent. There was no case of this as Mr. Mellor did not sue the newspapers but admitted his adultery and the newspapers themselves revealed that they had bugged the property.

Calcutt 2 proposed that the offence of breach of privacy would offer the individual the possibility of obtaining injunctions in the High Court to prevent publication of material gained in contravention of such a tort and damages against the newspapers to amount for any profit through publication of such material.

Another reason for such a privacy tort might be that as a European Community Member State, we must be reminded that our neighbours in France, Germany, Denmark and the Netherlands already have such a tort as does Canada in the United States of America.

THE RIGHT OF PRIVACY ALREADY IN THE LAW THAT PROTECTS AGAINST PRESS INTRUSION.

Before the Human Rights act 1998, UK law recognised no general right to privacy but the various areas of tort and equity such as trespass, breach of con-

---

4.   Kaye v Robertson & another [1990] The Times 21st March
      Editor and publishers of Sunday Sport appealed against injunction restraining them from publishing photos or statements which they obtained by unauthorised access to the plaintiff actor's room in hospital while he was a patient suffering from severe brain injuries and not fully in command of his faculties.
5.   Naomi Campbell v Mirror Group Newspapers Ltd [2002] EWCA Civ 1373
      This model had articles published about her attendance at meetings of Narcotics Anonymous . She had drug-related problems .

fidence, copyright and defamation are instances of a general right to privacy Article 8 of the Human Rights Act now applies (see APPENDIX)..
The case of *Douglas v Hello Magazine (2002)* [6]shows a common law recognition of privacy.
Intrusions on property are covered by trespass law Intrusions on persons are covered in the criminal law of nuisance. As regards nuisance on property, this involves disturbing a person in the enjoyment of his or her land to such an extent that the law regards this as unreasonable. So grossly invasive and embarrassing surveillance could

Amount to nuisance and be dealt with under criminal law already in force. as in the case of Khorasandjian v Bush (1993)[7] where an injunction was granted against the defendant to stop him from harassing, telephoning and generally pestering the plaintiff. In Hunter v Canary Wharf LTD (1997)[8] a House of Lords decision, it was decided that interference with television reception was capable of constituting a private nuisance and this over-ruled the previous case. In the Bush case, the person who sued for receiving harassing telephone calls was the child of the persons who owned the property she was in. In the Hunter case, Patricia Hunter was not the owner of the property, yet the Court gave a right in nuisance

These examples show that there are various areas of the law which exist and are aimed at the invasion of privacy and so already control the press in obtaining information about an individual's private life for the purpose of publication. The laws of confidence, copyright, defamation and malicious falsehood already control the publication of personal information. As regards the law of defamation, its only disadvantage in this respect is that the defence of justification means that it will not usually affect the situation when what is revealed are true facts as in the cases of Corelli v Wall (1906) [9]and Kaye v Robertson (1990)[10]

---

6. Douglas v Hello! [2002] EWHC 2560 (Ch)
7. Khorasandjian v Bush TLR 18.2/93, (1993) 3 All ER 669
8. Patricia Hunter & ors v Canary Wharf Ltd, House of Lords 24/4/97
9. Corelli v Wall (1906) 22 TLR 532. No action lay to restrain publication of postcards representing the plaintiff.
10. Gordon Kaye v Robertson & another TLR 21/3/90
    There was no right of action in restraining publication of statements and photographs obtained at unauthorised interview with actor.

BREACH OF CONFIDENCE AND PRESS FREEDOM

The case of Duchess of Argyll v Duke of Argyll(1965)[11] is an example of protection against public disclosure of personal information. The Duchess successfully sought an injunction to prohibit the Duke and a newspaper from publishing confidences she had divulged to her husband in the course of their marriage. But yet the decision was different in a similar case of Lennon v News Group Newspaper Ltd (1978) [12] when the former wife of John Lennon of the famous Beatles pop-group sold her story of her marriage to the News of the World newspaper who disclosed intimate details of the relationship between the plaintiff and his ex-wife. Lennon was denied an injunction because they were public PERSONALITIES.

CONFIDENCE IS THE AREA OF LAW WHICH OFFERS THE MOST EFFECTIVE PROTECTION OF PRIVACY.[13]

It has a broader scope than defamation. It is concerned with protecting confidentiality. In *Stevens v Avery (1988)* [14] information about sexual conduct was the subject of a duty of confidentiality.. The case concerned information communicated within a close friendship and it was not found necessary to identify a formal relationship between the parties at the time when the information was communicated. The information concerned the plaintiff's lesbian affair with a Mrs. Telling. On the facts, the disclosure of intimate details about someone's sexual life was held by Vice-Chancellor Browne-Wilkinson not to be trivial. He said "I have the greatest doubt whether wholesale revelation of the sexual conduct of an individual can properly be described as "trivial" tittle-tattle." He said "It is unconscionable for a person who has received information on the basis that it is confidential subsequently to reveal that information.. No particular pre-existing relationship is needed." From this, we can determine that breach of confidence law covers communication of confidential information by one complete stranger to another, as long as the communicator had informed the recipient that this information was confidential. This ruling is one way of protecting privacy.

---

11. Margaret, Duchess of Argyll v Duke of Argyll and others [1965] 1 All ER 611
12. Lennon v News Group Newspaper Ltd [1978] FSR 573
13. See the Younger Committee's report of 1972.
14. Stevens v Avery (1988) 2 WLR 1280

THE HUMAN RIGHTS ACT 1998 AND PRESS FREEDOM.

The Human Rights Act 1998 is the catalyst that will decide the privacy issue once case-law becomes less sparse on the matter. One case that develops the privacy issue is *Douglas v Hello! (2002)*[15] which was concerned with unauthorised photographs. Here the law of breach of confidence is shown to have the potential to develop into a full right of privacy.

In the case of *Venables v News Group Newspapers (2001)*, [16]injunctions were granted on the basis of confidentiality in the light of Article 10(see APPENDIX) Human Rights Act 1998.

Dame Elizabeth Butler-Sloss held that the court was obliged as a public authority to apply Article 10 to the case. She said that the Convention did not however create a free-standing course of action between private individuals but that the court had a duty to act compatibly with Convention rights. Her Ladyship felt that granting an injunction in this case fell within the restrictions of freedom of expression allowed by Article 10(2). The claimants' lives might be at risk if their identities were revealed, so the injunction had the effect of protecting their right to life under Article 2 (see APPENDIX)

As regards injunctions applied for to stop publication in the newspapers, Section 12 of the Appendix to the Human Rights Act now applies (see APPENDIX).

Conclusion

Various proposals have been put forward for a tort of breach of privacy in the UK. The trouble is that it would be difficult to achieve the right balance between privacy and Press freedom even if such a tort came onto the statute books. Section 12 of the Appendix to Human Rights Act 1998 requires the courts to give proper weight to freedom of expression when considering restraints of publication. It remains to be seen how the present regulatory bodies strike the balance between Article 8 and 10 of the Human Rights Act and

---

15. Douglas v Hello! [2002] EWHC 2560 (Ch)
16. Venables v News Group Newspapers LTR 14/10/2002: TLR 16/10/2002: ILR 18/10/2002-12-29
    In this case two young men who were serving sentences for the murder of a young boy, sought injunctions restraining the media from revealing information which would enable them to be identified once they were released from prison and given new identities.

whether there is a need for further statutory control by way of a new tort of breach of privacy.

Table of Cases

Attorney General v Times Newspapers	(1973) 3 All ER 54
Broadcasting Complaints Commission ex parte Granada Television Ltd	
	TLR 16/12/94
Campbell v MGN	[2002] EWCA Civ 1373
Corelli v Wall	(1906) 22 TLR 532
Douglas v Hello!	[2002]EWHC 2560 (Ch)
Duchess of Argyll v Duke of Argyll	[1967] Ch 302
Hunter v Canary Wharf Ltd	HL 24/4/97
Kaye v Roberson & another	TLR 21/3/90
Khorasandjian v Bush	(1993) 3 All ER 669
Lennon v News Group Newspapers Ltd	[1978] FSR 573
Stevens v Avery & others	(1988) FSR 510
Venables v News Group Newspapers Ltd	LTL 27/3/2002

Table of Statutes and Conventions

European Convention on Human Rights 1950
Human Rights Act 1998

Table of Reports, Codes, etc.

Broadcasting Standards Commission Code of Practice
Press Commission's Press Code
Press Complaints Commission Code of Practice

Bibliography

Cheyney.D,Dickson,.L,Fitzpatrick.J,Uglow.S; "Criminal Justice & the Human Rights Act 1998; (1999); Jordan Publishing Ltd.

Cowen.Z; "Cowen's Individual Liberty & The Law"; (1977); Oceana Publications

Freedom of Information Campaign Study (1980) ; Library Association Press

Jacobs.F.G,White.R.C.A; "The European Convention on Human Rights"; (1996); Clarendon Press

Liberty, editor of "Liberating Cyberspace"; (1999) Pluto Press

Reid.B.C; "Confidentiality and The Law"; (1986); Waterlow Publishers

Shattuck.J.H; "Rights of Privacy"; (1971); National Textbook Company

Wacks.R; "Personal Information"; (1989), Clarendon Press

Wacks.R; "Privacy & Press Freedom" (1995); Blackstone Press

Westin.A; "Privacy and Freedom"; (1967)

RELEVANT ARTICLES OF THE UK HUMAN RIGHTS ACT 1998

Article 2
Right to life.

1. Everyone's right to life shall be protected by law. No one shall be deprived of his life intentionally save in the execution of a sentence of a court following his conviction of a crime for which this penalty is provided by law.

2. Deprivation of life shall not be regarded as inflicted in contravention of this Article when it results from the use of force which is no more than absolutely necessary:

    a. in defence from any person from unlawful violence;

b.   in order to effect a lawful arrest or to prevent the escape of a person lawfully detained;

c.   in action lawfully taken for the purpose of quelling a riot or insurrection.

Article 8
Right to respect for private and family life.

1.   Everyone has the right to respect for his private and family life, his home and his correspondence.

2.   There shall be no interference by a public authority with the exercise of this right except such as in accordance with the law and is necessary in a democratic society in the interests of national security, public safety or the economic well-being of the country, for the prevention of disorder or crime, for the protection of health or morals, or for the protection of the rights and freedoms of others.

Article 10
Freedom of expression.

1.   Everyone has the right to freedom of expression. This right shall include freedom to hold opinions and to receive and impart information and ideas without interference by public authority and regardless of frontiers. This Article shall not prevent States from requiring the licensing of broadcasting, television or cinema enterprises.

2.   The exercise of these freedoms, since it carries with it duties and responsibilities, may be subject to such formalities, conditions, restrictions or penalties as are prescribed by law and are necessary in a democratic society, in the interests of national security, territorial integrity or public safety, for the prevention of disorder or crime, for the protection of health or morals, for the protection of the reputation or rights of others, for preventing the disclosure of information received in confidence, or for maintaining the authority and impartiality of the judiciary.

Appendix to the Human Rights Act 1998
Section 12. Freedom of expression.

(1) This section applies if a court is considering whether to grant any relief which, if granted, might affect the exercise of the Convention right to freedom of expression.

(2) The person against whom the application for relief is made (the respondent) is neither present nor represented, no such relief is to be granted unless the court is satisfied—

(a) that the applicant has taken all practical steps to notify the respondent; or

(b) that there are compelling reasons why the respondent should not be notified.

(1) No such relief is to be granted so as to restrain publication before trial unless the court is satisfied that the applicant is likely to establish that publication should not be allowed.

(2) The court must have particular regard to the importance of the Convention right to freedom of expression and, where the proceedings relate to material which the respondent claims, or which appears to the court, to be journalistic, literary or artistic material (or to conduct connected with such material), to—

(a) the extent to which—

(i) the material has, or is about to, become available to the public; or

(ii) it is, or would be, in the public interest for the material to be published;

(a) any relevant privacy code.

(1) In this section—
'court' includes a tribunal; and
'relief' includes any remedy or order (other than in criminal proceedings)

Bibliography

Cheyney.D, Dickson.L, Fitzpatrick.J, Uglow.S; "Criminal Justice & the Human Rights Act 1998; (1999) ; Jordan Publishing Ltd.

Cowen.Z; "Cowen's Individual Liberty & The Law"; (1977) ; Oceana Publications

Freedom of Information Campaign Study (1980) ; Library Association Press

Jacobs.F.G, White.R.C.A; "The European Convention on Human Rights"; (1996) ; Clarendon Press

Liberty, editor of "Liberating Cyberspace"; (1999) Pluto Press

Reid.B.C; "Confidentiality and The Law"; (1986) ; Waterlow Publishers

Shattuck.J.H; "Rights of Privacy"; (1971) ; National Textbook Company

Wacks.R; "Personal Information"; (1989), Clarendon Press

Wacks.R; "Privacy & Press Freedom" (1995) ; Blackstone Press

Westin.A; "Privacy and Freedom"; (1967)

Obscene Publications Act 1959

An Act to amend the law relating to the publication of obscene matter; to provide for the protection of literature; and to strengthen the law concerning pornography.

1 Test of obscenity

(1) For the purposes of this Act an article shall be deemed to be obscene if its effect or (where the article comprises two or more distinct items) the effect of any one of its items is, if taken as a whole, such as to tend to deprave and corrupt persons who are likely, having regard to all relevant circumstances, to read, see or hear the matter contained or embodied in it.

(2) In this Act "article" means any description of article containing or embodying matter to be read or looked at or both, any sound record, and any film or other record of a picture or pictures.

(3) For the purposes of this Act a person publishes an article who—

(a) distributes, circulates, sells, lets on hire, gives, or lends it, or who offers it for sale or for letting on hire; or

(b) in the case of an article containing or embodying matter to be looked at or a record, shows, plays or projects it[, or, where the matter is data stored electronically, transmits that data.]:

[(4) For the purposes of this Act a person also publishes an article to the extent that any matter recorded on it is included by him in a programme included in a programme service.

(5) Where the inclusion of any matter in a programme so included would, if that matter were recorded matter, constitute the publication of an obscene article for the purposes of this Act by virtue of subsection (4) above, this Act shall have effect in relation to the inclusion of that matter in that programme as if it were recorded matter.

(6) In this section "programme" and "programme service" have the same meaning as in the Broadcasting Act 1990.]

2 Prohibition of publication of obscene matter

(1) Subject as hereinafter provided, any person who, whether for gain or not publishes an obscene article [or who has an obscene article for publication for gain (whether gain to himself or gain to another)] shall be liable—

(a) on summary conviction to a fine not exceeding [the prescribed sum] or to imprisonment for a term not exceeding six months;

(b) on conviction on indictment to a fine or to imprisonment for a term not exceeding three years or both.

(2)…

(3) A prosecution…for an offence against this section shall not be commenced more than two years after the commission of the offence.

[(3A) Proceedings for an offence under this section shall not be instituted except by or with the consent of the Director of Public Prosecutions in any case where the article in question is a moving picture film of a width of not less than sixteen millimetres and the relevant publication or the only other publication which followed or could reasonably have been expected to follow from the relevant publication took place or (as the case may be) was to take place in the course of a *[film exhibition]* [an exhibition of a film]; and in this subsection "the relevant publication" means—

(a) in the case of any proceedings under this section for publishing an obscene article, the publication in respect of which the defendant would be charged if the proceedings were brought; and

(b) in the case of any proceedings under this section for having an obscene article for publication for gain, the publication which, if the proceedings were brought, the defendant would be alleged to have had in contemplation.]

(4) A person publishing an article shall not be proceeded against for an offence at common law consisting of the publication of any matter contained or embodied in the article where it is of the essence of the offence that the matter is obscene.

[(4A) Without prejudice to subsection (4) above, a person shall not be proceeded against for an offence at common law—

(a) in respect of *a* [film exhibition] [an exhibition of a film] or anything said or done in the course of *a* [film exhibition] [an exhibition of a film], where it is of the essence of the common law offence that the exhibition or, as the case may be, what was said or done was obscene, indecent, offensive, disgusting or injurious to morality; or

(b) in respect of an agreement to give *a [film exhibition]* [an exhibition of a film] or to cause anything to be said or done in the course of such an exhibition where the common law offence consists of conspiring to corrupt public morals or to do any act contrary to public morals or decency.]

(5) A person shall not be convicted of an offence against this section if he proves that he had not examined the article in respect of which he is charged and had no reasonable cause to suspect that it was such that his publication of it would make him liable to be convicted of an offence against this section.

(6) In any proceedings against a person under this section the question whether an article is obscene shall be determined without regard to any publication by another person unless it could reasonably have been expected that the publication by the other person would follow from publication by the person charged.

[(7) In this section "film exhibition" has the same meaning as in the Cinemas Act 1985.]

[(7) In this section, "exhibition of a film" has the meaning given in paragraph 15 of Schedule 1 to the Licensing Act 2003.]

3 Powers of search and seizure

(1) If a justice of the peace is satisfied by information on oath that there is reasonable ground for suspecting that, in any premises *in the petty sessions area for which he acts,* or on any stall or vehicle in that area, being premises or a stall or vehicle specified in the information, obscene articles are, or are from time to time, kept for publication for gain, the justice may issue a warrant under his hand empowering any constable to enter (if need be by force) and search the premises, or to search the stall or vehicle…and to seize and remove any articles found therein or thereon which the constable has reason to believe to be obscene articles and to be kept for publication for gain.

(2) A warrant under the foregoing subsection shall, if any obscene articles are seized under the warrant, also empower the seizure and removal of any documents found in the premises or, as the case may be, on the stall or vehicle which relate to a trade or business carried on at the premises or from the stall or vehicle.

(3) [Subject to subsection (3A) of this section] Any articles seized under subsection (1) of this section shall be brought before a justice of the peace acting *for the same petty sessions area as the justice who issued the warrant, and the justice before whom the articles are brought* [in the local justice area in which the articles

were seized, who] may thereupon issue a summons to the occupier of the premises or, as the case may be, the user of the stall or vehicle to appear on a day specified in the summons before a magistrates' court *for that petty sessions area* [acting in that local justice area] to show cause why the articles or any of them should not be forfeited; and if the court is satisfied, as respects any of the articles, that at the time when they were seized they were obscene articles kept for publication for gain, the court shall order those articles to be forfeited:
Provided that if the person summoned does not appear, the court shall not make an order unless service of the summons is proved.
[Provided also that this subsection does not apply in relation to any article seized under subsection (1) of this section which is returned to the occupier of the premises or, as the case may be, to the user of the stall or vehicle in or on which it was found.]
[(3A) Without prejudice to the duty of a court to make an order for the forfeiture of an article where section 1(4) of the Obscene Publications Act 1964 applies (orders made on conviction), in a case where by virtue of subsection (3A) of section 2 of this Act proceedings under the said section 2 for having an article for publication for gain could not be instituted except by or with the consent of the Director of Public Prosecutions, no order for the forfeiture of the article shall be made under this section unless the warrant under which the article was seized was issued on an information laid by or on behalf of the Director of Public Prosecutions.]

(4) In addition to the person summoned, any other person being the owner, author or maker of any of the articles brought before the court, or any other person through whose hands they had passed before being seized, shall be entitled to appear before the court on the day specified in the summons to show cause why they should not be forfeited.

(5) Where an order is made under this section for the forfeiture of any articles, any person who appeared, or was entitled to appear, to show cause against the making of the order may appeal to [the Crown Court]; and no such order shall take effect until the expiration of [the period within which notice of appeal to the Crown Court may be given against the order], or, if before the expiration thereof notice of appeal is duly given or application is made for the statement of a case for the opinion of the High Court, until the final determination or abandonment of the proceedings on the appeal or case.

(6) If as respects any articles brought before it the court does not order forfeiture, the court may if it thinks fit order the person on whose information the warrant for the seizure of the articles was issued to pay such costs as the court thinks reasonable to any person who has appeared before the court to show cause why those articles should not be forfeited; and costs ordered to be paid under this subsection shall be enforceable as a civil debt.

(7) For the purposes of this section the question whether an article is obscene shall be determined on the assumption that copies of it would be published in any manner likely having regard to the circumstances in which it was found, but in no other manner.

4 Defence of public good

(1) [Subject to subsection (1A) of this section] a person shall not be convicted of an offence against section two of this Act, and an order for forfeiture shall not be made under the foregoing section, if it is proved that publication of the article in question is justified as being for the public good on the ground that it is in the interests of science, literature, art or learning, or of other objects of general concern.

[(1A) Subsection (1) of this section shall not apply where the article in question is a moving picture film or soundtrack, but—

(a) a person shall not be convicted of an offence against section 2 of this Act in relation to any such film or soundtrack, and

(b) an order for forfeiture of any such film or soundtrack shall not be made under section 3 of this Act, if it is proved that publication of the film or soundtrack is justified as being for the public good on the ground that it is in the interests of drama, opera, ballet or any other art, or of literature or learning.]

(2) It is hereby declared that the opinion of experts as to the literary, artistic, scientific or other merits of an article may be admitted in any proceedings under this Act either to establish or to negative the said ground.

[(3) In this section "moving picture soundtrack" means any sound record designed for playing with a moving picture film, whether incorporated with the film or not.]

(1) This Act may be cited as the Obscene Publications Act 1959.

(2) This Act shall not extend to Scotland or to Northern Ireland.

Obscene Publications Act 1964

An Act to strengthen the law for preventing the publication for gain of obscene matter and the publication of things intended for the production of obscene matter

1 Obscene articles intended for publication for gain

(2) For the purpose of any proceedings for an offence against the said section 2 a person shall be deemed to have an article for publication for gain if with a view to such publication he has the article in his ownership, possession or control.

(3) In proceedings brought against a person under the said section 2 for having an obscene article for publication for gain the following provisions shall apply in place of subsections (5) and (6) of that section, that is to say,—

(a) he shall not be convicted of that offence if he proves that he had not examined the article and had no reasonable cause to suspect that it was such that his having it would make him liable to be convicted of an offence against that section; and

(b) the question whether the article is obscene shall be determined by reference to such publication for gain of the article as in the circumstances it may reasonably be inferred he had in contemplation and to any further publication that could reasonably be expected to follow from it, but not to any other publication.

(4) Where articles are seized under section 3 of the Obscene Publications Act 1959 (which provides for the seizure and forfeiture of obscene articles kept for publication for gain), and a person is convicted under section 2 of that Act of having them for publication for gain, the court on his conviction shall order the forfeiture of those articles:

Provided that an order made by virtue of this subsection (including an order so made on appeal) shall not take effect until the expiration of the ordinary time within which an appeal in the matter of the proceedings in which the order was made may be instituted or, where such an appeal is duly instituted, until the appeal is finally decided or abandoned; and for this purpose—

(a) an application for a case to be stated or for leave to appeal shall be treated as the institution of an appeal; and

(b) where a decision on appeal is subject to a further appeal, the appeal shall not be deemed to be finally decided until the expiration of the ordinary time within which a further appeal may be instituted or, where a further appeal is duly instituted, until the further appeal is finally decided or abandoned.

(5) References in section 3 of the Obscene Publications Act 1959 and this section to publication for gain shall apply to any publication with a view to gain, whether the gain is to accrue by way of consideration for the publication or in any other way.

2 Negatives, etc for production of obscene articles

(1) The Obscene Publications Act 1959 (as amended by this Act) shall apply in relation to anything which is intended to be used, either alone or as one of a set, for the reproduction or manufacture therefrom of articles containing or embodying matter to be read, looked at or listened to, as if it were an article containing or embodying that matter so far as that matter is to be derived from it or from the set.

(2) For the purposes of the Obscene Publications Act 1959 (as so amended) an article shall be deemed to be had or kept for publication if it is had or kept for the reproduction or manufacture therefrom of articles for publication; and the question whether an article so had or kept is obscene shall—

(a) for purposes of section 2 of the Act be determined in accordance with section 1(3)(*b*) above as if any reference there to publication of the article were a reference to publication of articles reproduced or manufactured from it; and

(b) for purposes of section 3 of the Act be determined on the assumption that articles reproduced or manufactured from it would be published in any manner likely having regard to the circumstances in which it was found, but in no other manner.

3 Citation, commencement and extent

(1) This Act may be cited as the Obscene Publications Act 1964, and this Act and the Obscene Publications Act 1959 may be cited together as the Obscene Publications Acts 1959 and 1964.

(2) This Act shall come into operation on the expiration of one month beginning with the date of the passing thereof.

(3) This Act shall not extend to Scotland or to Northern Ireland.

Human Rights Act 1998

An Act to give further effect to rights and freedoms guaranteed under the European Convention on Human Rights; to make provision with respect to holders of certain judicial offices who become judges of the European Court of Human Rights; and for connected purposes.

Introduction

1 The Convention Rights

(1) In this Act "the Convention rights" means the rights and fundamental freedoms set out in—
(a) Articles 2 to 12 and 14 of the Convention,
(b) Articles 1 to 3 of the First Protocol, and
(c) Articles 1 and 2 of the Sixth Protocol,
as read with Articles 16 to 18 of the Convention.
(2) Those Articles are to have effect for the purposes of this Act subject to any designated derogation or reservation (as to which see sections 14 and 15).
(3) The Articles are set out in Schedule 1.
(4) The [Secretary of State] may by order make such amendments to this Act as he considers appropriate to reflect the effect, in relation to the United Kingdom, of a protocol.
(5) In subsection (4) "protocol" means a protocol to the Convention—

(a) which the United Kingdom has ratified; or
(b) which the United Kingdom has signed with a view to ratification.
(6) No amendment may be made by an order under subsection (4) so as to come into force before the protocol concerned is in force in relation to the United Kingdom.

2 Interpretation of Convention rights

(1) A court or tribunal determining a question which has arisen in connection with a Convention right must take into account any—

(a) judgment, decision, declaration or advisory opinion of the European Court of Human Rights,

(b) opinion of the Commission given in a report adopted under Article 31 of the Convention,

(c) decision of the Commission in connection with Article 26 or 27(2) of the Convention, or

(d) decision of the Committee of Ministers taken under Article 46 of the Convention, whenever made or given, so far as, in the opinion of the court or tribunal, it is relevant to the proceedings in which that question has arisen.

(2) Evidence of any judgment, decision, declaration or opinion of which account may have to be taken under this section is to be given in proceedings before any court or tribunal in such manner as may be provided by rules.

(3) In this section "rules" means rules of court or, in the case of proceedings before a tribunal, rules made for the purposes of this section—

(a) by...the Secretary of State, in relation to any proceedings outside Scotland;

(b) by the Secretary of State, in relation to proceedings in Scotland; or

(c) by a Northern Ireland department, in relation to proceedings before a tribunal in Northern Ireland—

(i) which deals with transferred matters; and

(ii) for which no rules made under paragraph (a) are in force.

3 Interpretation of legislation

(1) So far as it is possible to do so, primary legislation and subordinate legislation must be read and given effect in a way which is compatible with the Convention rights.

(2) This section—

(a) applies to primary legislation and subordinate legislation whenever enacted;

(b) does not affect the validity, continuing operation or enforcement of any incompatible primary legislation; and

(c) does not affect the validity, continuing operation or enforcement of any incompatible subordinate legislation if (disregarding any possibility of revocation) primary legislation prevents removal of the incompatibility.

4 Declaration of incompatibility

(1) Subsection (2) applies in any proceedings in which a court determines whether a provision of primary legislation is compatible with a Convention right.

(2) If the court is satisfied that the provision is incompatible with a Convention right, it may make a declaration of that incompatibility.

(3) Subsection (4) applies in any proceedings in which a court determines whether a provision of subordinate legislation, made in the exercise of a power conferred by primary legislation, is compatible with a Convention right.

(4) If the court is satisfied—

(a) that the provision is incompatible with a Convention right, and

(b) that (disregarding any possibility of revocation) the primary legislation concerned prevents removal of the incompatibility, it may make a declaration of that incompatibility.

(5) In this section "court" means—

(a) the House of Lords;

(b) the Judicial Committee of the Privy Council;

(c) the Courts-Martial Appeal Court;

(d) in Scotland, the High Court of Justiciary sitting otherwise than as a trial court or the Court of Session;

(e) in England and Wales or Northern Ireland, the High Court or the Court of Appeal.

(6) A declaration under this section ("a declaration of incompatibility")—

(a) does not affect the validity, continuing operation or enforcement of the provision in respect of which it is given; and

(b) is not binding on the parties to the proceedings in which it is made.

5 Right of Crown to intervene

(1) Where a court is considering whether to make a declaration of incompatibility, the Crown is entitled to notice in accordance with rules of court.

(2) In any case to which subsection (1) applies—

(a) a Minister of the Crown (or a person nominated by him),

(b) a member of the Scottish Executive,

(c) a Northern Ireland Minister,

(d) a Northern Ireland department, is entitled, on giving notice in accordance with rules of court, to be joined as a party to the proceedings.

(3) Notice under subsection (2) may be given at any time during the proceedings.

(4) A person who has been made a party to criminal proceedings (other than in Scotland) as the result of a notice under subsection (2) may, with leave, appeal to the House of Lords against any declaration of incompatibility made in the proceedings.

(5) In subsection (4)—

"criminal proceedings" includes all proceedings before the Courts-Martial Appeal Court; and "leave" means leave granted by the court making the declaration of incompatibility or by the House of Lords. '

Transfer of Functions
6 Acts of public authorities

(1) It is unlawful for a public authority to act in a way which is incompatible with a Convention right.

(2) Subsection (1) does not apply to an act if—

(a) as the result of one or more provisions of primary legislation, the authority could not have acted differently; or

(b) in the case of one or more provisions of, or made under, primary legislation which cannot be read or given effect in a way which is compatible with the Convention rights, the authority was acting so as to give effect to or enforce those provisions.

(3) In this section "public authority" includes—

(a) a court or tribunal, and

(b) any person certain of whose functions are functions of a public nature, but does not include either House of Parliament or a person exercising functions in connection with proceedings in Parliament.

(4) In subsection (3) "Parliament" does not include the House of Lords in its judicial capacity.

(5) In relation to a particular act, a person is not a public authority by virtue only of subsection (3)(b) if the nature of the act is private.

(6) "An act" includes a failure to act but does not include a failure to—

(a) introduce in, or lay before, Parliament a proposal for legislation; or

(b) make any primary legislation or remedial order.

7 Proceedings

(1) A person who claims that a public authority has acted (or proposes to act) in a way which is made unlawful by section 6(1) may—

(a) bring proceedings against the authority under this Act in the appropriate court or tribunal, or

(b) rely on the Convention right or rights concerned in any legal proceedings, but only if he is (or would be) a victim of the unlawful act.

(2) In subsection (1)(a) "appropriate court or tribunal" means such court or tribunal as may be determined in accordance with rules; and proceedings against an authority include a counterclaim or similar proceeding.

(3) If the proceedings are brought on an application for judicial review, the applicant is to be taken to have a sufficient interest in relation to the unlawful act only if he is, or would be, a victim of that act.

(4) If the proceedings are made by way of a petition for judicial review in Scotland, the applicant shall be taken to have title and interest to sue in relation to the unlawful act only if he is, or would be, a victim of that act.

(5) Proceedings under subsection (1)(a) must be brought before the end of—

(a) the period of one year beginning with the date on which the act complained of took place; or

(b) such longer period as the court or tribunal considers equitable having regard to all the circumstances, but that is subject to any rule imposing a stricter time limit in relation to the procedure in question.

(6) In subsection (1)(b) "legal proceedings" includes—

(a) proceedings brought by or at the instigation of a public authority; and

(b) an appeal against the decision of a court or tribunal.

(7) For the purposes of this section, a person is a victim of an unlawful act only if he would be a victim for the purposes of Article 34 of the Convention if proceedings were brought in the European Court of Human Rights in respect of that act.

(8) Nothing in this Act creates a criminal offence.

(9) In this section "rules" means—

(a) in relation to proceedings before a court or tribunal outside Scotland, rules made by...the Secretary of State for the purposes of this section or rules of court,

(b) in relation to proceedings before a court or tribunal in Scotland, rules made by the Secretary of State for those purposes,

(c) in relation to proceedings before a tribunal in Northern Ireland—

(i) which deals with transferred matters; and

(ii) for which no rules made under paragraph (a) are in force, rules made by a Northern Ireland department for those purposes, and includes provision made by order under section 1 of the Courts and Legal Services Act 1990.

(10) In making rules, regard must be had to section 9.

(11) The Minister who has power to make rules in relation to a particular tribunal may, to the extent he considers it necessary to ensure that the tribunal can provide an appropriate remedy in relation to an act (or proposed act) of a public authority which is (or would be) unlawful as a result of section 6(1), by order add to—

(a) the relief or remedies which the tribunal may grant; or

(b) the grounds on which it may grant any of them.

(12) An order made under subsection (11) may contain such incidental, supplemental, consequential or transitional provision as the Minister making it considers appropriate.

(13) "The Minister" includes the Northern Ireland department concerned.

8 Judicial remedies

(1) In relation to any act (or proposed act) of a public authority which the court finds is (or would be) unlawful, it may grant such relief or remedy, or make such order, within its powers as it considers just and appropriate.

(2) But damages may be awarded only by a court which has power to award damages, or to order the payment of compensation, in civil proceedings.

(3) No award of damages is to be made unless, taking account of all the circumstances of the case, including—

(a) any other relief or remedy granted, or order made, in relation to the act in question (by that or any other court), and

(b) the consequences of any decision (of that or any other court) in respect of that act, the court is satisfied that the award is necessary to afford just satisfaction to the person in whose favour it is made.

(4) In determining—

(a) whether to award damages, or

(b) the amount of an award, the court must take into account the principles applied by the European Court of Human Rights in relation to the award of compensation under Article 41 of the Convention.

(5) A public authority against which damages are awarded is to be treated—

(a) in Scotland, for the purposes of section 3 of the Law Reform (Miscellaneous Provisions) (Scotland) Act 1940 as if the award were made in an action of damages in which the authority has been found liable in respect of loss or damage to the person to whom the award is made;

(b) for the purposes of the Civil Liability (Contribution) Act 1978 as liable in respect of damage suffered by the person to whom the award is made.

(6) In this section—

"court" includes a tribunal;

"damages" means damages for an unlawful act of a public authority; and

"unlawful" means unlawful under section 6(1).

9 Judicial acts

(1) Proceedings under section 7(1)(a) in respect of a judicial act may be brought only—

(a) by exercising a right of appeal;

(b) on an application (in Scotland a petition) for judicial review; or

(c) in such other forum as may be prescribed by rules.

(2) That does not affect any rule of law which prevents a court from being the subject of judicial review.

(3) In proceedings under this Act in respect of a judicial act done in good faith, damages may not be awarded otherwise than to compensate a person to the extent required by Article 5(5) of the Convention.

(4) An award of damages permitted by subsection (3) is to be made against the Crown; but no award may be made unless the appropriate person, if not a party to the proceedings, is joined.

(5) In this section—

"appropriate person" means the Minister responsible for the court concerned, or a person or government department nominated by him;

"court" includes a tribunal;

"judge" includes a member of a tribunal, a justice of the peace [(or, in Northern Ireland, a lay magistrate)] and a clerk or other officer entitled to exercise the jurisdiction of a court;

"judicial act" means a judicial act of a court and includes an act done on the instructions, or on behalf, of a judge; and

"rules" has the same meaning as in section 7(9).

10 Power to take remedial action

(1) This section applies if—

(a) a provision of legislation has been declared under section 4 to be incompatible with a Convention right and, if an appeal lies—

(i) all persons who may appeal have stated in writing that they do not intend to do so;

(ii) the time for bringing an appeal has expired and no appeal has been brought within that time; or

(iii) an appeal brought within that time has been determined or abandoned; or

(b) it appears to a Minister of the Crown or Her Majesty in Council that, having regard to a finding of the European Court of Human Rights made after the coming into force of this section in proceedings against the United Kingdom, a provision of legislation is incompatible with an obligation of the United Kingdom arising from the Convention.

(2) If a Minister of the Crown considers that there are compelling reasons for proceeding under this section, he may by order make such amendments to the legislation as he considers necessary to remove the incompatibility.

(3) If, in the case of subordinate legislation, a Minister of the Crown considers—

(a) that it is necessary to amend the primary legislation under which the subordinate legislation in question was made, in order to enable the incompatibility to be removed, and

(b) that there are compelling reasons for proceeding under this section, he may by order make such amendments to the primary legislation as he considers necessary.

(4) This section also applies where the provision in question is in subordinate legislation and has been quashed, or declared invalid, by reason of incompatibility with a Convention right and the Minister proposes to proceed under paragraph 2(b) of Schedule 2.

(5) If the legislation is an Order in Council, the power conferred by subsection (2) or (3) is exercisable by Her Majesty in Council.

(6) In this section "legislation" does not include a Measure of the Church Assembly or of the General Synod of the Church of England.

(7) Schedule 2 makes further provision about remedial orders.

11 Safeguard for existing human rights

A person's reliance on a Convention right does not restrict—

(a) any other right or freedom conferred on him by or under any law having effect in any part of the United Kingdom; or

(b) his right to make any claim or bring any proceedings which he could make or bring apart from sections 7 to 9.

12 Freedom of expression

(1) This section applies if a court is considering whether to grant any relief which, if granted, might affect the exercise of the Convention right to freedom of expression.

(2) If the person against whom the application for relief is made ("the respondent") is neither present nor represented, no such relief is to be granted unless the court is satisfied—

(a) that the applicant has taken all practicable steps to notify the respondent; or

(b) that there are compelling reasons why the respondent should not be notified.

(3) No such relief is to be granted so as to restrain publication before trial unless the court is satisfied that the applicant is likely to establish that publication should not be allowed.

(4) The court must have particular regard to the importance of the Convention right to freedom of expression and, where the proceedings relate to material which the respondent claims, or which appears to the court, to be journalistic, literary or artistic material (or to conduct connected with such material), to—

(a) the extent to which—

(i) the material has, or is about to, become available to the public; or

(ii) it is, or would be, in the public interest for the material to be published;

(b) any relevant privacy code.

(5) In this section—

"court" includes a tribunal; and

"relief" includes any remedy or order (other than in criminal proceedings).

13 Freedom of thought, conscience and religion

(1) If a court's determination of any question arising under this Act might affect the exercise by a religious organisation (itself or its members collectively) of the Convention right to freedom of thought, conscience and religion, it must have particular regard to the importance of that right.

(2) In this section "court" includes a tribunal.

14 Derogations

(1) In this Act "designated derogation" means—

any derogation by the United Kingdom from an Article of the Convention, or of any protocol to the Convention, which is designated for the purposes of this Act in an order made by the [Secretary of State].

(2) ommitted

(3) If a designated derogation is amended or replaced it ceases to be a designated derogation.

(4) But subsection (3) does not prevent the [Secretary of State] from exercising his power under subsection (1)…to make a fresh designation order in respect of the Article concerned.

(5) The [Secretary of State] must by order make such amendments to Schedule 3 as he considers appropriate to reflect—

(a) any designation order; or

(b) the effect of subsection (3).

(6) A designation order may be made in anticipation of the making by the United Kingdom of a proposed derogation.

15 Reservations

(1) In this Act "designated reservation" means—

(a) the United Kingdom's reservation to Article 2 of the First Protocol to the Convention; and

(b) any other reservation by the United Kingdom to an Article of the Convention, or of any protocol to the Convention, which is designated for the purposes of this Act in an order made by the [Secretary of State].

(2) The text of the reservation referred to in subsection (1)(a) is set out in Part II of Schedule 3.

(3) If a designated reservation is withdrawn wholly or in part it ceases to be a designated reservation.

(4) But subsection (3) does not prevent the [Secretary of State] from exercising his power under subsection (1)(b) to make a fresh designation order in respect of the Article concerned.

(5) The [Secretary of State] must by order make such amendments to this Act as he considers appropriate to reflect—

(a) any designation order; or

(b) the effect of subsection (3).

16 Period for which designated derogations have effect

(1) If it has not already been withdrawn by the United Kingdom, a designated derogation ceases to have effect for the purposes of this Act—
at the end of the period of five years beginning with the date on which the order designating it was made.
(2) At any time before the period—
(a) fixed by subsection (1)…, or
(b) extended by an order under this subsection, comes to an end, the [Secretary of State] may by order extend it by a further period of five years.
(3) An order under section 14(1)…ceases to have effect at the end of the period for consideration, unless a resolution has been passed by each House approving the order.
(4) Subsection (3) does not affect—
(a) anything done in reliance on the order; or
(b) the power to make a fresh order under section 14(1)….
(5) In subsection (3) "period for consideration" means the period of forty days beginning with the day on which the order was made.
(6) In calculating the period for consideration, no account is to be taken of any time during which—
(a) Parliament is dissolved or prorogued; or

(b) both Houses are adjourned for more than four days.
(7) If a designated derogation is withdrawn by the United Kingdom, the [Secretary of State] must by order make such amendments to this Act as he considers are required to reflect that withdrawal.

17 Periodic review of designated reservations

(1) The appropriate Minister must review the designated reservation referred to in section 15(1)(a)—
(a) before the end of the period of five years beginning with the date on which section 1(2) came into force; and
(b) if that designation is still in force, before the end of the period of five years beginning with the date on which the last report relating to it was laid under subsection (3).
(2) The appropriate Minister must review each of the other designated reservations (if any)—

(a) before the end of the period of five years beginning with the date on which the order designating the reservation first came into force; and

(b) if the designation is still in force, before the end of the period of five years beginning with the date on which the last report relating to it was laid under subsection (3).

(3) The Minister conducting a review under this section must prepare a report on the result of the review and lay a copy of it before each House of Parliament.

18 Appointment to European Court of Human Rights

(1) In this section "judicial office" means the office of—

(a) Lord Justice of Appeal, Justice of the High Court or Circuit judge, in England and Wales;

(b) judge of the Court of Session or sheriff, in Scotland;

(c) Lord Justice of Appeal, judge of the High Court or county court judge, in Northern Ireland.

(2) The holder of a judicial office may become a judge of the European Court of Human Rights ("the Court") without being required to relinquish his office.

(3) But he is not required to perform the duties of his judicial office while he is a judge of the Court.

(4) In respect of any period during which he is a judge of the Court—

(a) a Lord Justice of Appeal or Justice of the High Court is not to count as a judge of the relevant court for the purposes of section 2(1) or 4(1) of the Supreme Court Act 1981 (maximum number of judges) nor as a judge of the Supreme Court for the purposes of section 12(1) to (6) of that Act (salaries etc);

(b) a judge of the Court of Session is not to count as a judge of that court for the purposes of section 1(1) of the Court of Session Act 1988 (maximum number of judges) or of section 9(1)(c) of the Administration of Justice Act 1973 ("the 1973 Act") (salaries etc);

(c) a Lord Justice of Appeal or judge of the High Court in Northern Ireland is not to count as a judge of the relevant court for the purposes of section 2(1) or 3(1) of the Judicature (Northern Ireland) Act 1978 (maximum number of judges) nor as a judge of the Supreme Court of Northern Ireland for the purposes of section 9(1)(d) of the 1973 Act (salaries etc);

(d) a Circuit judge is not to count as such for the purposes of section 18 of the Courts Act 1971 (salaries etc);

(e) a sheriff is not to count as such for the purposes of section 14 of the Sheriff Courts (Scotland) Act 1907 (salaries etc);

(f) a county court judge of Northern Ireland is not to count as such for the purposes of section 106 of the County Courts Act (Northern Ireland) 1959 (salaries etc).

(5) If a sheriff principal is appointed a judge of the Court, section 11(1) of the Sheriff Courts (Scotland) Act 1971 (temporary appointment of sheriff principal) applies, while he holds that appointment, as if his office is vacant.

(6) Schedule 4 makes provision about judicial pensions in relation to the holder of a judicial office who serves as a judge of the Court.

(7) The Lord Chancellor or the Secretary of State may by order make such transitional provision (including, in particular, provision for a temporary increase in the maximum number of judges) as he considers appropriate in relation to any holder of a judicial office who has completed his service as a judge of the Court.

19 Statements of compatibility

(1) A Minister of the Crown in charge of a Bill in either House of Parliament must, before Second Reading of the Bill—

(a) make a statement to the effect that in his view the provisions of the Bill are compatible with the Convention rights ("a statement of compatibility"); or

(b) make a statement to the effect that although he is unable to make a statement of compatibility the government nevertheless wishes the House to proceed with the Bill.

(2) The statement must be in writing and be published in such manner as the Minister making it considers appropriate.

20 Orders etc under this Act

(1) Any power of a Minister of the Crown to make an order under this Act is exercisable by statutory instrument.

(2) The power of…the Secretary of State to make rules (other than rules of court) under section 2(3) or 7(9) is exercisable by statutory instrument.

(3) Any statutory instrument made under section 14, 15 or 16(7) must be laid before Parliament.

(4) No order may be made by…the Secretary of State under section 1(4), 7(11) or 16(2) unless a draft of the order has been laid before, and approved by, each House of Parliament.

(5) Any statutory instrument made under section 18(7) or Schedule 4, or to which subsection (2) applies, shall be subject to annulment in pursuance of a resolution of either House of Parliament.

(6) The power of a Northern Ireland department to make—

(a) rules under section 2(3)(c) or 7(9)(c), or

(b) an order under section 7(11), is exercisable by statutory rule for the purposes of the Statutory Rules (Northern Ireland) Order 1979.

(7) Any rules made under section 2(3)(c) or 7(9)(c) shall be subject to negative resolution; and section 41(6) of the Interpretation Act (Northern Ireland) 1954 (meaning of "subject to negative resolution") shall apply as if the power to make the rules were conferred by an Act of the Northern Ireland Assembly.

(8) No order may be made by a Northern Ireland department under section 7(11) unless a draft of the order has been laid before, and approved by, the Northern Ireland Assembly.

21 Interpretation, etc

(1) In this Act—

"amend" includes repeal and apply (with or without modifications);

"the appropriate Minister" means the Minister of the Crown having charge of the appropriate authorised government department (within the meaning of the Crown Proceedings Act 1947);

"the Commission" means the European Commission of Human Rights;

"the Convention" means the Convention for the Protection of Human Rights and Fundamental Freedoms, agreed by the Council of Europe at Rome on 4th November 1950 as it has effect for the time being in relation to the United Kingdom;

"declaration of incompatibility" means a declaration under section 4;

"Minister of the Crown" has the same meaning as in the Ministers of the Crown Act 1975;

"Northern Ireland Minister" includes the First Minister and the deputy First Minister in Northern Ireland;

"primary legislation" means any—

(a) public general Act;

(b) local and personal Act;

(c) private Act;

(d) Measure of the Church Assembly;

(e) Measure of the General Synod of the Church of England;

(f) Order in Council—

(i) made in exercise of Her Majesty's Royal Prerogative;

(ii) made under section 38(1)(a) of the Northern Ireland Constitution Act 1973 or the corresponding provision of the Northern Ireland Act 1998; or

(iii) amending an Act of a kind mentioned in paragraph (a), (b) or (c);

and includes an order or other instrument made under primary legislation (otherwise than by the National Assembly for Wales, a member of the Scottish Executive, a Northern Ireland Minister or a Northern Ireland department) to the extent to which it operates to bring one or more provisions of that legislation into force or amends any primary legislation;

"the First Protocol" means the protocol to the Convention agreed at Paris on 20th March 1952;

"the Sixth Protocol" means the protocol to the Convention agreed at Strasbourg on 28th April 1983;

"the Eleventh Protocol" means the protocol to the Convention (restructuring the control machinery established by the Convention) agreed at Strasbourg on 11th May 1994;

"remedial order" means an order under section 10;

"subordinate legislation" means any—

(a) Order in Council other than one—

(i) made in exercise of Her Majesty's Royal Prerogative;

(ii) made under section 38(1)(a) of the Northern Ireland Constitution Act 1973 or the corresponding provision of the Northern Ireland Act 1998; or

(iii) amending an Act of a kind mentioned in the definition of primary legislation;

(b) Act of the Scottish Parliament;

(c) Act of the Parliament of Northern Ireland;

(d) Measure of the Assembly established under section 1 of the Northern Ireland Assembly Act 1973;

(e) Act of the Northern Ireland Assembly;

(f) order, rules, regulations, scheme, warrant, byelaw or other instrument made under primary legislation (except to the extent to which it operates to bring one or more provisions of that legislation into force or amends any primary legislation);

(g) order, rules, regulations, scheme, warrant, byelaw or other instrument made under legislation mentioned in paragraph (b), (c), (d) or (e) or made under an Order in Council applying only to Northern Ireland;

(h) order, rules, regulations, scheme, warrant, byelaw or other instrument made by a member of the Scottish Executive, a Northern Ireland Minister or a

Northern Ireland department in exercise of prerogative or other executive functions of Her Majesty which are exercisable by such a person on behalf of Her Majesty;

"transferred matters" has the same meaning as in the Northern Ireland Act 1998; and "tribunal" means any tribunal in which legal proceedings may be brought.

(2) The references in paragraphs (b) and (c) of section 2(1) to Articles are to Articles of the Convention as they had effect immediately before the coming into force of the Eleventh Protocol.

(3) The reference in paragraph (d) of section 2(1) to Article 46 includes a reference to Articles 32 and 54 of the Convention as they had effect immediately before the coming into force of the Eleventh Protocol.

(4) The references in section 2(1) to a report or decision of the Commission or a decision of the Committee of Ministers include references to a report or decision made as provided by paragraphs 3, 4 and 6 of Article 5 of the Eleventh Protocol (transitional provisions).

(5) Any liability under the Army Act 1955, the Air Force Act 1955 or the Naval Discipline Act 1957 to suffer death for an offence is replaced by a liability to imprisonment for life or any less punishment authorised by those Acts; and those Acts shall accordingly have effect with the necessary modifications.

22 Short title, commencement, application and extent

(1) This Act may be cited as the Human Rights Act 1998.

(2) Sections 18, 20 and 21(5) and this section come into force on the passing of this Act.

(3) The other provisions of this Act come into force on such day as the Secretary of State may by order appoint; and different days may be appointed for different purposes.

(4) Paragraph (b) of subsection (1) of section 7 applies to proceedings brought by or at the instigation of a public authority whenever the act in question took place; but otherwise that subsection does not apply to an act taking place before the coming into force of that section.

(5) This Act binds the Crown.

(6) This Act extends to Northern Ireland.

(7) Section 21(5), so far as it relates to any provision contained in the Army Act 1955, the Air Force Act 1955 or the Naval Discipline Act 1957, extends to any place to which that provision extends.

Part I
The Convention Rights and Freedoms

Article 2

1

Everyone's right to life shall be protected by law. No one shall be deprived of his life intentionally save in the execution of a sentence of a court following his conviction of a crime for which this penalty is provided by law.

2

Deprivation of life shall not be regarded as inflicted in contravention of this Article when it results from the use of force which is no more than absolutely necessary:

(a) in defence of any person from unlawful violence;

(b) in order to effect a lawful arrest or to prevent the escape of a person lawfully detained;

(c) in action lawfully taken for the purpose of quelling a riot or insurrection.

Article 3
Prohibition of torture

No one shall be subjected to torture or to inhuman or degrading treatment or punishment.

Article 4
Prohibition of slavery and forced labour

1 No one shall be held in slavery or servitude.

2 No one shall be required to perform forced or compulsory labour.

3 For the purpose of this Article the term "forced or compulsory labour" shall not include:

(a) any work required to be done in the ordinary course of detention imposed according to the provisions of Article 5 of this Convention or during conditional release from such detention;

(b) any service of a military character or, in case of conscientious objectors in countries where they are recognised, service exacted instead of compulsory military service;

(c) any service exacted in case of an emergency or calamity threatening the life or well-being of the community;

(d) any work or service which forms part of normal civic obligations.

Article 5
Right to liberty and security

1

Everyone has the right to liberty and security of person. No one shall be deprived of his liberty save in the following cases and in accordance with a procedure prescribed by law:

(a) the lawful detention of a person after conviction by a competent court;

(b) the lawful arrest or detention of a person for non-compliance with the lawful order of a court or in order to secure the fulfilment of any obligation prescribed by law;

(c) the lawful arrest or detention of a person effected for the purpose of bringing him before the competent legal authority on reasonable suspicion of having committed an offence or when it is reasonably considered necessary to prevent his committing an offence or fleeing after having done so;

(d) the detention of a minor by lawful order for the purpose of educational supervision or his lawful detention for the purpose of bringing him before the competent legal authority;

(e) the lawful detention of persons for the prevention of the spreading of infectious diseases, of persons of unsound mind, alcoholics or drug addicts or vagrants;

(f) the lawful arrest or detention of a person to prevent his effecting an unauthorised entry into the country or of a person against whom action is being taken with a view to deportation or extradition.

2

Everyone who is arrested shall be informed promptly, in a language which he understands, of the reasons for his arrest and of any charge against him.

3

Everyone arrested or detained in accordance with the provisions of paragraph 1(c) of this Article shall be brought promptly before a judge or other officer authorised by law to exercise judicial power and shall be entitled to trial within a reasonable time or to release pending trial. Release may be conditioned by guarantees to appear for trial.

4.

Everyone who is deprived of his liberty by arrest or detention shall be entitled to take proceedings by which the lawfulness of his detention shall be decided speedily by a court and his release ordered if the detention is not lawful.

5

Everyone who has been the victim of arrest or detention in contravention of the provisions of this Article shall have an enforceable right to compensation.

Article 6
Right to a fair trial

1

In the determination of his civil rights and obligations or of any criminal charge against him, everyone is entitled to a fair and public hearing within a reasonable time by an independent and impartial tribunal established by law. Judgment shall be pronounced publicly but the press and public may be excluded from all or part of the trial in the interest of morals, public order or national security in a democratic society, where the interests of juveniles or the protection of the private life of the parties so require, or to the extent strictly necessary in the opinion of the court in special circumstances where publicity would prejudice the interests of justice.

2

Everyone charged with a criminal offence shall be presumed innocent until proved guilty according to law.

3

Everyone charged with a criminal offence has the following minimum rights:

(a) to be informed promptly, in a language which he understands and in detail, of the nature and cause of the accusation against him;

(b) to have adequate time and facilities for the preparation of his defence;

(c) to defend himself in person or through legal assistance of his own choosing or, if he has not sufficient means to pay for legal assistance, to be given it free when the interests of justice so require;

(d) to examine or have examined witnesses against him and to obtain the attendance and examination of witnesses on his behalf under the same conditions as witnesses against him;

(e) to have the free assistance of an interpreter if he cannot understand or speak the language used in court.

Article 7
No punishment without law

1

No one shall be held guilty of any criminal offence on account of any act or omission which did not constitute a criminal offence under national or international

law at the time when it was committed. Nor shall a heavier penalty be imposed than the one that was applicable at the time the criminal offence was committed.
2
This Article shall not prejudice the trial and punishment of any person for any act or omission which, at the time when it was committed, was criminal according to the general principles of law recognised by civilised nations.

Article 8
Right to respect for private and family life

1
Everyone has the right to respect for his private and family life, his home and his correspondence.
2
There shall be no interference by a public authority with the exercise of this right except such as is in accordance with the law and is necessary in a democratic society in the interests of national security, public safety or the economic well-being of the country, for the prevention of disorder or crime, for the protection of health or morals, or for the protection of the rights and freedoms of others.

Article 9
Freedom of thought, conscience and religion

1
Everyone has the right to freedom of thought, conscience and religion; this right includes freedom to change his religion or belief and freedom, either alone or in community with others and in public or private, to manifest his religion or belief, in worship, teaching, practice and observance.
2
Freedom to manifest one's religion or beliefs shall be subject only to such limitations as are prescribed by law and are necessary in a democratic society in the interests of public safety, for the protection of public order, health or morals, or for the protection of the rights and freedoms of others.

Article 10
Freedom of expression

1
Everyone has the right to freedom of expression. This right shall include freedom to hold opinions and to receive and impart information and ideas without

interference by public authority and regardless of frontiers. This Article shall not prevent States from requiring the licensing of broadcasting, television or cinema enterprises.

2

The exercise of these freedoms, since it carries with it duties and responsibilities, may be subject to such formalities, conditions, restrictions or penalties as are prescribed by law and are necessary in a democratic society, in the interests of national security, territorial integrity or public safety, for the prevention of disorder or crime, for the protection of health or morals, for the protection of the reputation or rights of others, for preventing the disclosure of information received in confidence, or for maintaining the authority and impartiality of the judiciary.

Article 11
Freedom of assembly and association

1

Everyone has the right to freedom of peaceful assembly and to freedom of association with others, including the right to form and to join trade unions for the protection of his interests.

2

No restrictions shall be placed on the exercise of these rights other than such as are prescribed by law and are necessary in a democratic society in the interests of national security or public safety, for the prevention of disorder or crime, for the protection of health or morals or for the protection of the rights and freedoms of others. This Article shall not prevent the imposition of lawful restrictions on the exercise of these rights by members of the armed forces, of the police or of the administration of the State.

Article 12
Right to marry

Men and women of marriageable age have the right to marry and to found a family, according to the national laws governing the exercise of this right.

Article 14
Prohibition of discrimination

The enjoyment of the rights and freedoms set forth in this Convention shall be secured without discrimination on any ground such as sex, race, colour, language, religion, political or other opinion, national or social origin, association with a national minority, property, birth or other status.

Article 16
Restrictions on political activity of aliens

Nothing in Articles 10, 11 and 14 shall be regarded as preventing the High Contracting Parties from imposing restrictions on the political activity of aliens.

Article 17
Prohibition of abuse of rights

Nothing in this Convention may be interpreted as implying for any State, group or person any right to engage in any activity or perform any act aimed at the destruction of any of the rights and freedoms set forth herein or at their limitation to a greater extent than is provided for in the Convention.

Article 18
Limitation on use of restrictions on rights

The restrictions permitted under this Convention to the said rights and freedoms shall not be applied for any purpose other than those for which they have been prescribed.

Part II
The First Protocol

Article 1
Protection of property

Every natural or legal person is entitled to the peaceful enjoyment of his possessions. No one shall be deprived of his possessions except in the public interest and subject to the conditions provided for by law and by the general principles of international law.
The preceding provisions shall not, however, in any way impair the right of a State to enforce such laws as it deems necessary to control the use of property in accordance with the general interest or to secure the payment of taxes or other contributions or penalties.

Article 2
Right to education

No person shall be denied the right to education. In the exercise of any functions which it assumes in relation to education and to teaching, the State shall respect the right of parents to ensure such education and teaching in conformity with their own religious and philosophical convictions.

Article 3
Right to free elections

The High Contracting Parties undertake to hold free elections at reasonable intervals by secret ballot, under conditions which will ensure the free expression of the opinion of the people in the choice of the legislature.

Part III
The Sixth Protocol

Article 1
Abolition of the death penalty

The death penalty shall be abolished. No one shall be condemned to such penalty or executed.

Article 2
Death penalty in time of war

A State may make provision in its law for the death penalty in respect of acts committed in time of war or of imminent threat of war; such penalty shall be applied only in the instances laid down in the law and in accordance with its provisions. The State shall communicate to the Secretary General of the Council of Europe the relevant provisions of that law.

SCHEDULE 2
REMEDIAL ORDERS

Orders

1
(1) A remedial order may—

(a) contain such incidental, supplemental, consequential or transitional provision as the person making it considers appropriate;

(b) be made so as to have effect from a date earlier than that on which it is made;

(c) make provision for the delegation of specific functions;

(d) make different provision for different cases.

(2) The power conferred by sub-paragraph (1)(a) includes—

(a) power to amend primary legislation (including primary legislation other than that which contains the incompatible provision); and

(b) power to amend or revoke subordinate legislation (including subordinate legislation other than that which contains the incompatible provision).

(3) A remedial order may be made so as to have the same extent as the legislation which it affects.

(4) No person is to be guilty of an offence solely as a result of the retrospective effect of a remedial order.

Procedure

2

No remedial order may be made unless—

(a) a draft of the order has been approved by a resolution of each House of Parliament made after the end of the period of 60 days beginning with the day on which the draft was laid; or

(b) it is declared in the order that it appears to the person making it that, because of the urgency of the matter, it is necessary to make the order without a draft being so approved.

Orders laid in draft

3

(1) No draft may be laid under paragraph 2(a) unless—

(a) the person proposing to make the order has laid before Parliament a document which contains a draft of the proposed order and the required information; and

(b) the period of 60 days, beginning with the day on which the document required by this sub-paragraph was laid, has ended.

(2) If representations have been made during that period, the draft laid under paragraph 2(a) must be accompanied by a statement containing—

(a) a summary of the representations; and

(b) if, as a result of the representations, the proposed order has been changed, details of the changes.

Urgent cases

4

(1) If a remedial order ("the original order") is made without being approved in draft, the person making it must lay it before Parliament, accompanied by the required information, after it is made.

(2) If representations have been made during the period of 60 days beginning with the day on which the original order was made, the person making it must (after the end of that period) lay before Parliament a statement containing—

(a) a summary of the representations; and

(b) if, as a result of the representations, he considers it appropriate to make changes to the original order, details of the changes.

(3) If sub-paragraph (2)(b) applies, the person making the statement must—

(a) make a further remedial order replacing the original order; and

(b) lay the replacement order before Parliament.

(4) If, at the end of the period of 120 days beginning with the day on which the original order was made, a resolution has not been passed by each House approving the original or replacement order, the order ceases to have effect (but without that affecting anything previously done under either order or the power to make a fresh remedial order).

Definitions

In this Schedule—

"representations" means representations about a remedial order (or proposed remedial order) made to the person making (or proposing to make) it and includes any relevant Parliamentary report or resolution; and "required information" means—

(a) an explanation of the incompatibility which the order (or proposed order) seeks to remove, including particulars of the relevant declaration, finding or order; and

(b) a statement of the reasons for proceeding under section 10 and for making an order in those terms.

Calculating periods

6

In calculating any period for the purposes of this Schedule, no account is to be taken of any time during which—

(a) Parliament is dissolved or prorogued; or

(b) both Houses are adjourned for more than four days.

[**7**

(1) This paragraph applies in relation to—

(a) any remedial order made, and any draft of such an order proposed to be made,—

(i) by the Scottish Ministers; or

(ii) within devolved competence (within the meaning of the Scotland Act 1998) by Her Majesty in Council; and

(b) any document or statement to be laid in connection with such an order (or proposed order).

(2) This Schedule has effect in relation to any such order (or proposed order), document or statement subject to the following modifications.

(3) Any reference to Parliament, each House of Parliament or both Houses of Parliament shall be construed as a reference to the Scottish Parliament.

(4) Paragraph 6 does not apply and instead, in calculating any period for the purposes of this Schedule, no account is to be taken of any time during which the Scottish Parliament is dissolved or is in recess for more than four days.]

SCHEDULE 3
DEROGATION AND RESERVATION
Sections 14 and 15
Part I

[Part
I
Derogation]

Public emergency in the United Kingdom

The terrorist attacks in New York, Washington, DC and Pennsylvania on 11th September 2001 resulted in several thousand deaths, including many

British victims and others from 70 different countries. In its resolutions 1368 (2001) and 1373 (2001), the United Nations Security Council recognised the attacks as a threat to international peace and security.

The threat from international terrorism is a continuing one. In its resolution 1373 (2001), the Security Council, acting under Chapter VII of the United Nations Charter, required all States to take measures to prevent the commission of terrorist attacks, including by denying safe haven to those who finance, plan, support or commit terrorist attacks.

There exists a terrorist threat to the United Kingdom from persons suspected of involvement in international terrorism. In particular, there are foreign nationals present in the United Kingdom who are suspected of being concerned in the commission, preparation or instigation of acts of international terrorism, of being members of organisations or groups which are so concerned or of having links with members of such organisations or groups, and who are a threat to the national security of the United Kingdom.

As a result, a public emergency, within the meaning of Article 15(1) of the Convention, exists in the United Kingdom.

The Anti-terrorism, Crime and Security Act 2001

As a result of the public emergency, provision is made in the Anti-terrorism, Crime and Security Act 2001, inter alia, for an extended power to arrest and detain a foreign national which will apply where it is intended to remove or deport the person from the United Kingdom but where removal or deportation is not for the time being possible, with the consequence that the detention would be unlawful under existing domestic law powers. The extended power to arrest and detain will apply where the Secretary of State issues a certificate indicating his belief that the person's presence in the United Kingdom is a risk to national security and that he suspects the person of being an international terrorist. That certificate will be subject to an appeal to the Special Immigration Appeals Commission ("SIAC"), established under the Special Immigration Appeals Commission Act 1997, which will have power to cancel it if it considers that the certificate should not have been issued. There will be an appeal on a point of law from a ruling by SIAC. In addition, the certificate will be reviewed by SIAC at regular intervals. SIAC will also be able to grant bail, where appropriate, subject to conditions. It will be open to a detainee to end his detention at any time by agreeing to leave the United Kingdom.

The extended power of arrest and detention in the Anti-terrorism, Crime and Security Act 2001 is a measure which is strictly required by the exigencies of the situation. It is a temporary provision which comes into force for an initial period of 15 months and then expires unless renewed by Parliament. Thereafter, it is subject to annual renewal by Parliament. If, at any time, in the Government's assessment, the public emergency no longer exists or the extended power is no longer strictly required by the exigencies of the situation, then the Secretary of State will, by Order, repeal the provision.

Domestic law powers of detention (other than under the Anti-terrorism, Crime and Security Act 2001)

The Government has powers under the Immigration Act 1971 ("the 1971 Act") to remove or deport persons on the ground that their presence in the United Kingdom is not conducive to the public good on national security grounds. Persons can also be arrested and detained under Schedules 2 and 3 to the 1971 Act pending their removal or deportation. The courts in the United Kingdom have ruled that this power of detention can only be exercised during the period necessary, in all the circumstances of the particular case, to effect removal and that, if it becomes clear that removal is not going to be possible within a reasonable time, detention will be unlawful (*R v Governor of Durham Prison, ex parte Singh* [1984] 1A11 ER 983).

Article 5(1)(f) of the Convention

It is well established that Article 5(1)(f) permits the detention of a person with a view to deportation only in circumstance where "action is being taken with a view to deportation" (*Chahal v United Kingdom* (1996) 23 EHRR 413 at paragraph 112). In that case the European Court of Human Rights indicated that detention will cease to be permissible under Article 5(1)(f) if deportation proceedings are not prosecuted with due diligence and that it was necessary in such cases to determine whether the duration of the deportation proceedings was excessive (paragraph 113).

In some cases, where the intention remains to remove or deport a person on national security grounds, continued detention may not be consistent with

Article 5(1)(f) as interpreted by the Court in the *Chahal* case. This may be the case, for example, if the person has established that removal to their own country might result in treatment contrary to Article 3 of the Convention. In such circumstances, irrespective of the gravity of the threat to national security posed by the person concerned, it is well established that Article 3 prevents removal or deportation to a place where there is a real risk that the person will suffer treatment contrary to that article. If no alternative destination is immediately available then removal or deportation may not, for the time being, be possible even though the ultimate intention remains to remove or deport the person once satisfactory arrangements can be made. In addition, it may not be possible to prosecute the person for a criminal offence given the strict rules on the admissibility of evidence in the criminal justice system of the United Kingdom and the high standard of proof required.

Derogation under Article 15 of the Convention

The Government has considered whether the exercise of the extended power to detain contained in the Anti-terrorism, Crime and Security Act 2001 may be inconsistent with the obligations under Article 5(1) of the Convention. As indicated above, there may be cases where, notwithstanding a continuing intention to remove or deport a person who is being detained, it is not possible to say that "action is being taken with a view to deportation" within the meaning of Article 5(1)(f) as interpreted by the Court in the *Chahal* case. To the extent, therefore, that the exercise of the extended power may be inconsistent with the United Kingdom's obligations under Article 5(1), the Government has decided to avail itself of the right of derogation conferred by Article 15(1) of the Convention and will continue to do so until further notice.

SCHEDULE 4
JUDICIAL PENSIONS
Section 18(6)

Duty to make orders about pensions

1

(1) The appropriate Minister must by order make provision with respect to pensions payable to or in respect of any holder of a judicial office who serves as an ECHR judge.

(2) A pensions order must include such provision as the Minister making it considers is necessary to secure that—

(3)

(a) an ECHR judge who was, immediately before his appointment as an ECHR judge, a member of a judicial pension scheme is entitled to remain as a member of that scheme;

(b) the terms on which he remains a member of the scheme are those which would have been applicable had he not been appointed as an ECHR judge; and

(c) entitlement to benefits payable in accordance with the scheme continues to be determined as if, while serving as an ECHR judge, his salary was that which would (but for section 18(4)) have been payable to him in respect of his continuing service as the holder of his judicial office.

Contributions

2

A pensions order may, in particular, make provision—

(a for any contributions which are payable by a person who remains a member of a scheme as a result of the order, and which would otherwise be payable by deduction from his salary, to be made otherwise than by deduction from his salary as an ECHR judge; and

(b) for such contributions to be collected in such manner as may be determined by the administrators of the scheme.

Amendments of other enactments

3

A pensions order may amend any provision of, or made under, a pensions Act in such manner and to such extent as the Minister making the order considers necessary or expedient to ensure the proper administration of any scheme to which it relates.

Definitions

4

In this Schedule—

"appropriate Minister" means—

(a) in relation to any judicial office whose jurisdiction is exercisable exclusively in relation to Scotland, the Secretary of State; and

(b) otherwise, the Lord Chancellor;

"ECHR judge" means the holder of a judicial office who is serving as a judge of the Court;

"judicial pension scheme" means a scheme established by and in accordance with a pensions Act;

"pensions Act" means—

(a) the County Courts Act (Northern Ireland) 1959;

(b) the Sheriffs' Pensions (Scotland) Act 1961;

(c) the Judicial Pensions Act 1981; or

(d) the Judicial Pensions and Retirement Act 1993; and

"pensions order" means an order made under paragraph 1.

END

0-595-32427-4

www.ingramcontent.com/pod-product-compliance
Lightning Source LLC
Chambersburg PA
CBHW030756180526
45163CB00003B/1043